Favorite Songs of the Nineties
Complete Original Sheet Music
for 89 Songs

Edited by
Robert A. Fremont

With an Introduction by Max Morath

Dover Publications, Inc.
New York

Published in Canada by General Publishing Company, Ltd., 30 Lesmill Road, Don Mills, Toronto, Ontario.
Published in the United Kingdom by Constable and Company, Ltd., 10 Orange Street, London WC 2.

Favorite Songs of the Nineties is a new work, first published by Dover Publications, Inc., in 1973. It consists of unabridged, unaltered republications of the sheet music for 89 popular songs (original publishers and dates of publication are indicated in the Contents). The work also contains an Editor's Preface and an Introduction by Max Morath.

International Standard Book Number: 0-486-21536-9
Library of Congress Catalog Card Number: 72-92765

Manufactured in the United States of America
Dover Publications, Inc.
180 Varick Street
New York, N.Y. 10014

Editor's Preface

Favorite Songs of the Nineties contains the best and most enduring popular songs written from the mid-1880's to the middle of the first decade of the new century. These songs are the ones that most people today still enjoy and still want to play and sing. Songs like "After the Ball," "Daisy Bell," "The Sidewalks of New York," "Give My Regards to Broadway," "The Band Played On," "Bill Bailey, Won't You Please Come Home?" and 83 others of equal quality and familiarity will always be popular as long as people enjoy singing together.

To my knowledge, this volume represents the most comprehensive collection of songs from the Nineties available today, and the only one that reproduces the original (or very early) sheet publications of these desirable songs. This is the way these pieces were performed when they were brand new. You are likely to be surprised at the differences that decades of popular interpretation have introduced in words and sometimes in the turn of a tune. Since the originals reproduced here are faithful historical documents as well as sources of enjoyment, the lyrics and artwork have not been changed even in the half-dozen instances where they reflect the broader humor of their less sophisticated era, in which the nation was far less sensitive to jibes about minority groups. The handful of songs so affected have not been tampered with, in the belief that a mature understanding of our past is more fruitful than a "double-think" falsification of history.

For his generous permission to reproduce all these items from his fabulous personal collection of rare sheet music, Dover Publications owes Mr. William Lloyd Keepers a debt of thanks. In addition, Mr. Keepers' advice and keen musical knowledge of the period have greatly influenced this work.

I also want to thank Messrs. Hayward Cirker, Everett Bleiler and Stanley Appelbaum of Dover Publications for their encouragement and suggestions, as well as the Lincoln Center Library Special Collections staff for assistance with my research. Finally, I want to thank my parents for filling our home with music, and my wife Vicki, who listened to these and many other songs on our home piano, and made the project great fun for our whole family.

R. A. F.

Introduction

The Era

The Nineties!

Already it is difficult to separate fact from myth—a difficulty that's inevitable, I suppose. Who can encompass, what most careful observer can capture, the glorious chaos of any year-span, much less that yeasty American decade moving into the twentieth century?

But we try. And in trying, we simplify. Being pattern-loving, pigeon-holing creatures cherishing order and continuity, we divide history into "eras"; we label our decades, alliteratively if possible. (Will the Seventies be Sensuous or Severe? Or Superfluous?) Nostalgia—history as-pablum —must especially be packaged neatly, each generation assigned the memories on which it must unflaggingly dote, reflexively scorning the popular culture both fore and aft of its own. (This process, relying on media, accelerates. The "Good Old Days" will soon be last summer. The Beatles, as this is written, are already certified nostalgia.)

So we have the Nineties—"Naughty" the alliterative adjective, "Gay" the most hackneyed, "Mauve Decade" having had a brief vogue after the publication of Thomas Beer's book by that name. For me not one of them works. I just can't write off that explosive decade with a quick flick of the late-late-show wrist, as if it could really have been the contradictory world of cancans and crinoline that Alice Faye and Jack Oakie told me it was.

So if you're expecting a syrupy preface awash with nostalgia, flip on by to "After the Ball" and start your sight-reading. Ditto if you expect the opposite—a condescending put-down of those campy and preposterous songs our grandmothers and grandfathers sang around the parlor piano and somehow managed to take *seriously*. Unfair. I've studied the popular songs from the 1880's to the present for years. And I long ago got used to the fact that 99% of anything "pop" is imitative and ephemeral, is essentially a form of fashion, and as such, sets deadly traps for those who attempt its premature evaluation as art.

But this only deepens my fascination. First, I want to know about the men and women behind these songs—the flesh and blood that wrote and sang and printed and pushed until, out of the welter of doggerel produced during these pristine years of pop, some eighty-odd songs managed to hang on long enough in the national consciousness to make it into this 1972 collection.

Then, I am intensively challenged (and charmed) by the era that spawned the music. I want to know about it.

And I don't view it as your average era. It was chosen, *marked*.

I propose a new delineation for it—still over-simplified, but at least rejecting the pop-history fiat that the story of human affairs must somehow divide itself into gum-labeled decades, solely because man has chosen to number the earth's revolutions around the sun by the decimal system. As a bracketing with logic behind it, how about the "Exposition Era"? Columbian Exposition, Chicago, to Louisiana Purchase Exposition, St. Louis. Outside dates, 1892–1904. Neat.

For these were the fairest of Fairs. They hit the public awareness with the impact of rockets fired from the rollercoaster. Today's American, surfeited, bored with the ballyhoo of progress from every side, cannot possibly imagine the stunned elations of America at Fair time. *Exposition Era!* The Time of the Fairs. I submit it's a sensible stab at a self-defining period in our national life. And with a World's Fair at each end and a war in the middle, it is beautifully in character.

The war of course was a shabby affair, so depicted, I'll remind you, not only in smug retrospect, but by many leading voices of the time, including Mark Twain and Finley Peter Dunne's Mr. Dooley. But it was sold to the public as a stirring and patriotic exercise befitting a great nation now moving with nineteenth-century European-colonial certainty toward Empire. The spunky average American of those days should have known better and many did. The military romance known as the "Spanish-American" war (plus the Philippine "insurrection" and the Boxer affair in China—we enjoyed almost continuous military orgasm for about five years) went almost unnoticed, for instance, by the song writers. They would flood the market a few years later with chains of ditties about the "Great War" of 1917–18. But now, except for cashing in occasionally on the Civil War with a belated blue-and-gray threnody such as "Break the News to Mother," they shunned the wars and stayed with courtship, home and mother as primary song conceits. That they by-passed the "Splendid Little War" out of moral indignation, however, is not certain; they may have reached unspoken agreement that it wouldn't sell. (Only one hit song, "A Hot Time in the Old Town," is associated with the war, having become the unofficial marching song of the troops. This must have furnished a few laughs to the sports in the district at St. Louis, where the song had originated some years earlier, the "hot time" referring to a different form of combat.)

But the Fairs were far more important to us and to history than the war. Both Fairs were huge magnets that drew musicians and entertainers from all over America to the plentiful gigs on the midway and in the high-paying resorts and saloons that flourished alongside the fairgrounds. Both Fairs were of main-chance importance to itinerant black and white pianists and minstrels. Seeds of syncopation, planted in the hotbeds of Chicago, matured in St. Louis ten years later as full-grown ragtime. Scott Joplin worked both Fairs; John Philip Sousa conducted "After the Ball" at the Chicago Fair. Topical songs about all this abounded, and one for each Fair can be found in this collection: "Streets of Cairo" (for Chicago) and "Meet Me in St. Louis." But that's all just for fun. There was a deeper influence.

Vastly more important is the idea of the Fairs as a symbol of the coming of age of America. It was a coming of age unique and painfully different; it had never happened to any nation before; it would never happen again in just this way. This polyglot, energized, on-the-make population, unbound on this most bountiful continent, *at this time* in history, preening itself, showing off to itself and the world, now saw the future through the crystal expanses along the midway. The Fairs were the signs out

front advertising a whole new line of goods inside.

Come to the Fair! See the new lines that will change the world! Electric lights and phonographs, wireless telegraphy, kinetoscopes soon to be full-fledged movies, autos, telephones, snapshot cameras, even (some had heard) flying machines—in short, the whole line of hardware that has in the span of this uncompleted century changed the face of life and set us on a no-turning-back course.

So began, if you will, *media*. Where it will end nobody knows but it began here, and that is overwhelmingly important.

I know "media" is a tricky word, a loaded word, but it's in vogue, and it's the only word we have for that set of technological forces which now melded with man's uneven efforts in arts and letters to send them booming around the world. Maybe *extensions* is a better word. Modern man had learned to extend his senses. He had learned to capture sound, capture images, preserve both, transmit both around the world and thence to infinity. *Extensions.*

The change happened in a wink, really—in those few years spanning the century's turning, a split second of historical time. Our time. So the songs in this collection were the first to spread themselves through this new web of technological extension—recorded, mass-printed and promoted, illustrated with colored slides, punched into piano rolls, endlessly performed in tandem with silent movies at the nickelodeons. No wonder music became an industry. In one generation that most intimate, most vulnerable and hesitant act—writing a song—became the stuff of technicians and board chairmen.

The Exposition Era connected two worlds. At least half these songs reflect the still insular world of the composer's childhood. These men, born by candlelight into a world where cultural immortality depended on memory and barely circulated print, died under electric lights, the scratchy phonograph records of their often frail songs destined now to echo down through the centuries ahead. The songsmith's dream had come true. He would be heard forever. And these, our minstrels, were the first. Extended by technology, they are the first pop immortals.

The Songs and Their Composers

It is not straining musical history to say that until about 1890, there was no such thing as "popular" music.

Of course there had been music publishers before. There were those old and stately Boston and New York firms, their catalogs quietly disclosing chaste art songs and études under sterile and be-curlicued covers; and there were hundreds of tiny, foredoomed, *ad hoc* com-

panies, their offices usually no wider than the hatbands of their owners, entering the publishing business with a thousand copies of a hopeful two-step or polka by the town's leading bandsman. But popular music was destined to become big business, and that meant organization, promotion, *sales*. The old-time publishers just couldn't measure up.

By a happy coincidence the first song in this book's alphabetical arrangement is "After the Ball," the Charles K. Harris ballad that emerged as the first real "popular song," i.e. big seller. Published in 1892 after its successful inclusion in the smash stage vehicle *A Trip to Chinatown*, "After the Ball" made financial if not artistic history. It eventually sold upwards of 5,000,000 copies, and it signaled the beginning of the now media-readied race for the sheet music and phonograph record bonanzas, those new and seemingly bottomless mines of pop music loot. Remembering that it couldn't have happened without all those inventions of "extension" (media), it is vastly interesting now to study the men themselves and their rampaging new business, which somehow took the name (or was it the place of business?), "Tin Pan Alley."

Seeds of art reposed in the catalogs of the awkward new publishing giants, if the full blossoms did not. In the work of George M. Cohan the new shape of musical theater was taking form—brisk, salty, raggy with irreverence, *American*. From Victor Herbert, the first "real" musician to venture into popular music, the theater received another injection of genius and innovation. It would all soon coalesce in the full-blown American musical, a really new kind of musical theater. Irving Berlin and Jerome Kern were already waiting in the wings.

If germinal theater music is well represented in this collection, what of that most essentially American music, jazz? Or, since our first-decade date-boundary obviously puts us too early, what of the jazz predecessors, ragtime and blues?

The strongest musical flux from the black world of turn-of-the-century America was certainly the unstoppable tide of ragtime, led by performer-writers like Scott Joplin, Ben Harney, James Scott, Tony Jackson and countless forgotten and nameless "men of color." This collection makes no attempt to include piano ragtime, although much of the best of it coincides precisely with the period we cover here. But you will certainly find the exciting new drive of ragtime in "Bill Bailey." And you'll get a whiff of it in "Coax Me" and "Teasing." (Musically, I mean. But read on. The saucy lyrics are probably rag-generated too.) Bob Cole, a black composer, is represented here with "Under the Bamboo Tree," a landmark tune vastly successful in its own time, relentlessly raggy in words and music and endlessly fun to play and sing.

"Bailey" and "Bamboo Tree" are the closest we come in this anthology to that dismal category of material from this period known as "coon" songs. Some were set to superb rag accompaniments; many were hits; measured by sales figures and general popularity, they should be included here. But on the basis of taste and decency the coon song deserves, not tribute in reprint, but ostracism to the back shelves in the dusty Museum of Pop. Examine its viciousness and condescension there, if you're curious, or if you can view this aspect of an earlier America with scholarly detachment.

Oddly though, an influence of the coon song transcending its racial slur and dialect is operating in many of the song lyrics of this collection. Syncopating and musically free, the coon song loosened language for the song writer generally; it licensed his use of slang and colloquialism, even bad grammar. This liberation spanned the years of our collection, so you can see it in action. Compare (philologically) the corseted "She May Have Seen Better Days" with the convivial "Forty-five Minutes from Broadway."

A strange and more subtle phenomenon of language and emotion shift was also taking place. The hard-core coon song ascribed to the Negro laziness, cowardice, unbridled sentimentality and, in deepest-wounding caricature, a pratfall love life. But laziness, cowardice, bathos, a love life of tragicomedy are, after all, the lot of all men. So as the coon song entrenched itself in popular music, it began to speak for Everyman from behind its burnt-cork mask. Recognizing ourselves, we could laugh or cry without embarrassment, transferring uncomfortable sentiments to black surrogates in song and play.

In another musical tide at the turn of the century, the blues of the black world were ready to break into print and thus into popular music, so to put it through another set of changes harmonically, lyrically, socially. "Baby Seals Blues" would be the first published, in 1912, and with W. C. Handy in the vanguard, the blues rush would be on. You'll search in vain, though, for even a hint of the blues in any of these hits pre-1907, so you'll be forced to speculate: how deep in the underground were the blues? Or, were they there at all?

On yet another musical front, talented young black writers were coming up alongside Berlin and Kern: Joe Jordan, the brilliantly versatile Eubie Blake and his partner Noble Sissle, Bert Williams and his talented group of writers. They would head for the theater with their music, following Bob Cole and his co-composers Rosamond and James Weldon Johnson, with full kits of classic/folk/blues/ragtime tools.

Joplin, Handy, Williams, Blake, Cole, the Johnsons, theirs was the toughest struggle of all, their accomplishments ten times as difficult, because of the prejudice they met, their influence (viewed as you choose—either as racial tradition or as the work of a remarkable set of individual geniuses, or both) the deepest and most significant of all.

Most of the songs in this collection were written by *troubadours*—or minstrels (in the original sense of the word). That is, the men (and women) presented here were singers first, composers second. Some, like Harry

Von Tilzer, began careers on stage, then exited as song-writing success came. Others, notably George M. Cohan, James Thornton, Gus Edwards, continued long and productive lives wearing both hats—performer's and composer's.

Admittedly, change was in the air. That sturdy pro Victor Herbert was working the full-fledged composer's beat—conducting the orchestra of course, but definitely not working any vaudeville turns. And as the harbinger of another Tin Pan Alley type, song-writer-as-businessman, Charles K. Harris blazed the trail as he hung out his first shingle in Milwaukee at age eighteen: "Charles K. Harris—Songs Written to Order."

Song writing was soon to become a full-time profession. The composer who sang would limit his vocalizing to professional sessions at his publisher's office or to an occasional solo at the corner bar.

But, as a morsel for your rumination, please note that today, our writers are, again, our singers (well-staffed, it must be said, with lawyers and accountants). The trou-

badours have returned—Nilsson, Baez, Lennon and Mc-Cartney, King, St. Marie, Simon. Does it mean anything? Is James Taylor related, artistically, to James Thornton? Carol King to Carrie Jacobs-Bond?

Consider, as you ruminate, some words by Isaac Goldberg in his *Tin Pan Alley*, looking back from 1930 at the milieu of our gaudy '90's, which ". . . attracted a type of minstrel who cried in earnest over his humble ditties— who philosophized like a weeping Carpenter—who sang sermons to the Good Life and smiled at Fortune. To sing, even the lowest type of ribald song, to versify, even the most patent doggerel, is to take wing, if but for a moment, above the material concerns of earth."

Perhaps—in grand and glorious contradiction to the things-will-never-be-the-same-again pop/media juggernaut I have so carefully laid on above—perhaps a singer must simply sing his songs. Perhaps all are eternally *troubadours,* transcending time and technique.

MAX MORATH

Contents

The songs are arranged in strict alphabetical order by their original titles as printed on the sheets (not counting "A" or "The" at the beginning of a title). Well-known alternate titles are included in this table of contents in the form of unnumbered cross references (e.g., *"East Side, West Side:* see *The Sidewalks of New York"*). For each song the following information is given when available: title (lyricist, composer), publisher of the sheet reprinted here [generally the original publisher, except for European imports and cases of transferred ownership], the city in which that publisher's office was located, the year(s) of copyright [sometimes of composition—not necessarily the year of printing of the particular sheet reproduced here]. Where titles or composers' names appear in different forms in different parts of a given sheet, this table of contents attempts to give the most correct or reliable form.

Contents

Contents

Contents

After The Ball

BY CHAS. K. HARRIS,

... AUTHOR OF ...

"BREAK THE NEWS TO MOTHER," "'MID THE GREEN FIELDS OF VIRGINIA," "HELLO CENTRAL GIVE ME HEAVEN," "I'VE A LONGING IN MY HEART FOR YOU, LOUISE," "FOR OLD TIMES' SAKE." ETC., ETC.

5

PUBLISHED BY
CHAS·K·HARRIS
NEW YORK
CHICAGO
CANADIAN-AMERICAN MUSIC CC. L'T'D.-TORONTO, CANADA.
CHAS. SHEARD & CO. LONDON.
AUSTRALIAN OFFICE, ALBERT & SON 137-139 KING ST. SYDNEY.

FREDERICK POLLWORTH & BRO., MUSIC PRINTERS, MILWAUKEE.

AFTER THE BALL.

Arr. by JOS. CLAUDER.

Words and Music by CHAS. K. HARRIS.

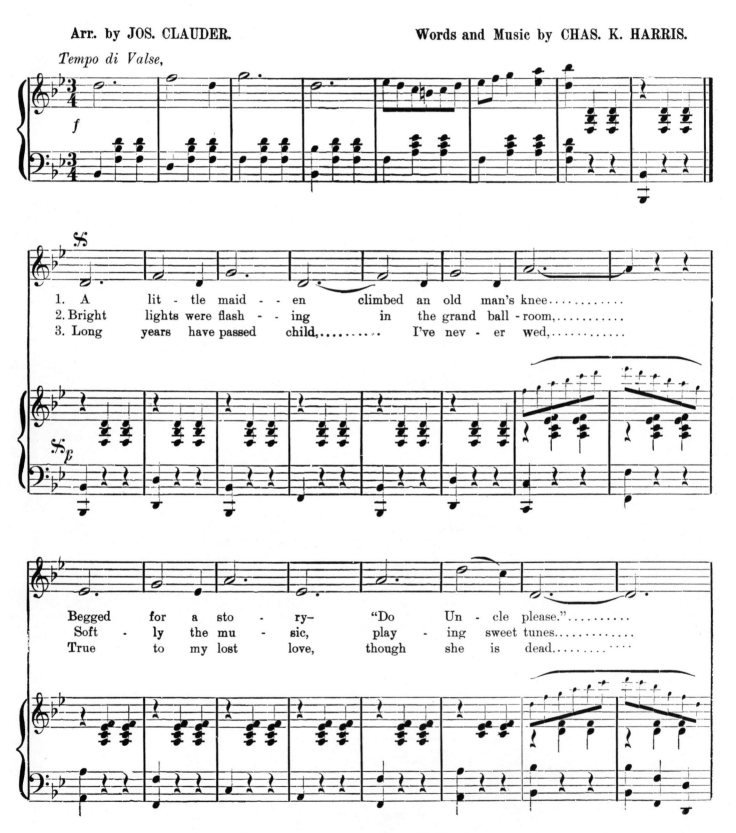

1. A lit - tle maid - - en climbed an old man's knee............
2. Bright lights were flash - - ing in the grand ball - room,...........
3. Long years have passed child,......... I've nev - er wed,............

Begged for a sto - ry- "Do Un - cle please."..........
Soft - ly the mu - sic, play - ing sweet tunes.............
True to my lost love, though she is dead.........

Where she is now pet, you will soon know.........
Kiss - ing my sweet - heart as lov - ers can.........
He was her broth - er— the let - ter ran.........

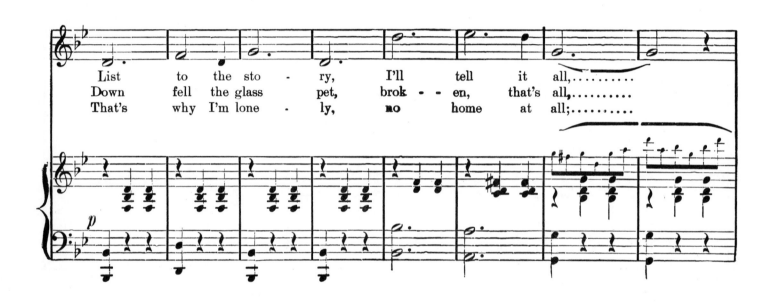

List to the sto - ry, I'll tell it all,.........
Down fell the glass pet, brok - - en, that's all,.........
That's why I'm lone - ly, no home at all;.........

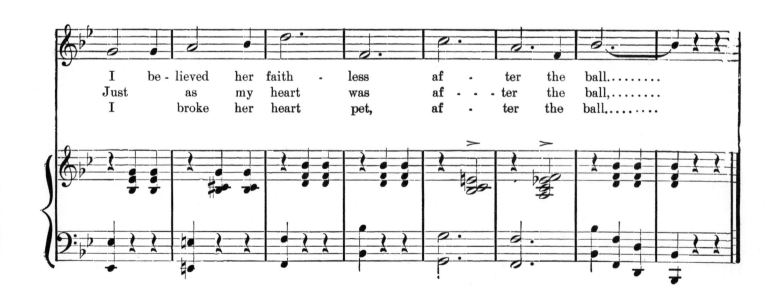

I be - lieved her faith - less af - ter the ball.........
Just as my heart was af - - ter the ball,.........
I broke her heart pet, af - ter the ball.........

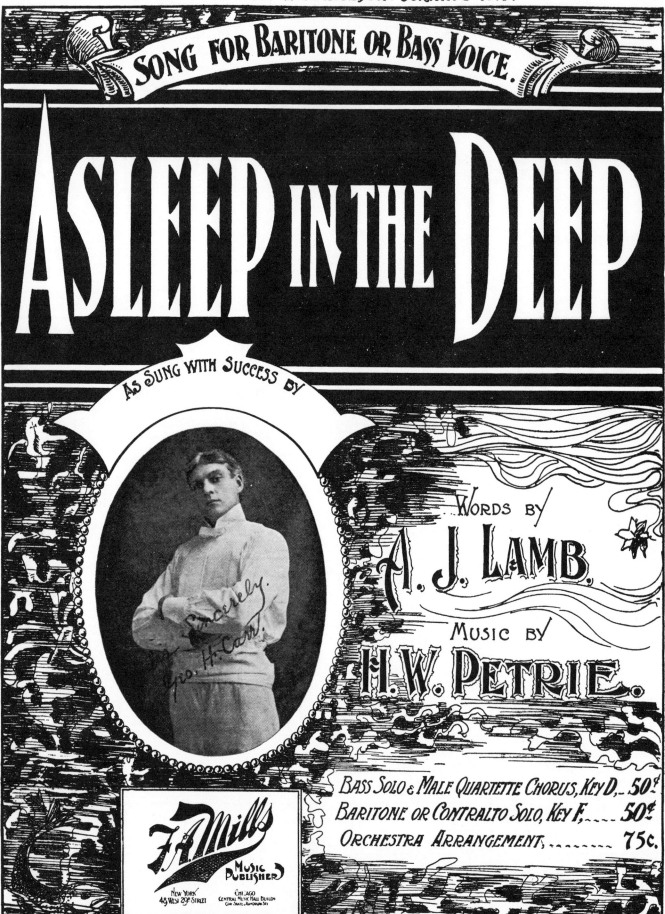

"Asleep in the Deep."

(BARITONE OR CONTRALTO.)

This song is also published in the key of D,
As a Bass Solo and Male Quartette Chorus.

Words by ARTHUR J. LAMB.

Music by H. W. PETRIE.

INTRODUCTION.

1. Storm-y the night and the waves roll high, Brave-ly the ship doth ride;........
2. What of the storm when the night is o'er? There is no trace or sign!........

REFRAIN.

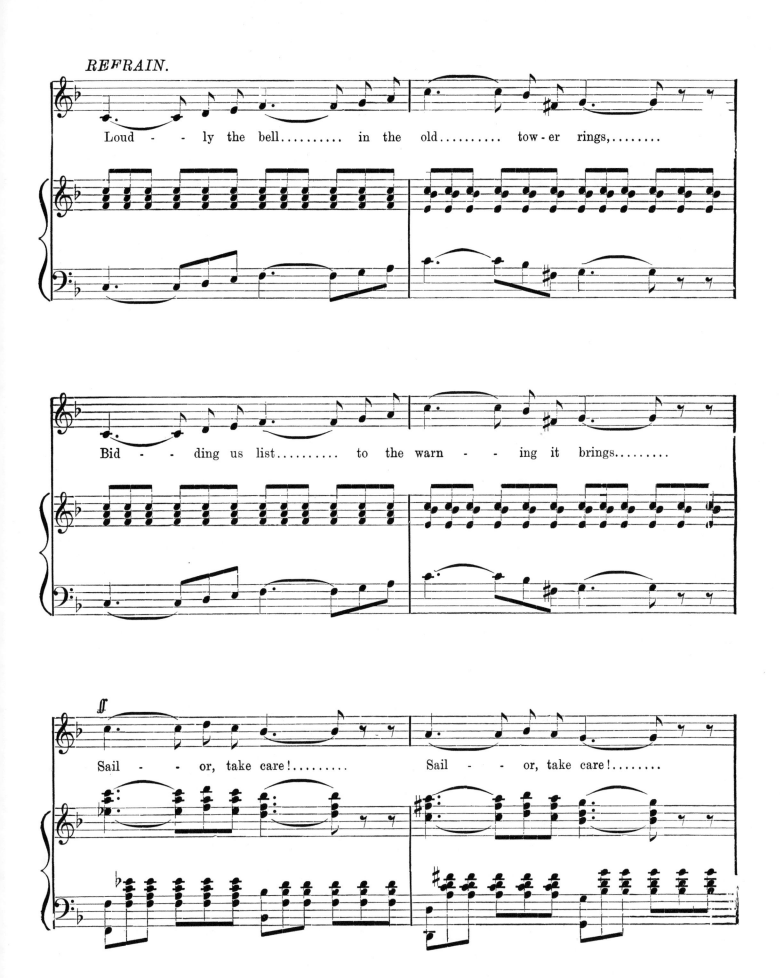

Loud - - ly the bell......... in the old......... tow - er rings,........

Bid - - ding us list......... to the warn - - ing it brings........

Sail - - or, take care!........ Sail - - or, take care!........

AS SUNG AT THE FUNERAL OF OUR MARTYRED PRESIDENT
WILLIAM McKINLEY
BY THE EUTERPEAN QUARTETTE

BEAUTIFUL ISLE OF SOMEWHERE

A SOPRANO SOLO
WITH ORGAN OR PIANO
ACCOMPANIMENT

A QUARTETTE FOR
MEN'S VOICES

A QUARTETTE FOR
WOMEN'S VOICES

ALL THREE ARRANGEMENTS
IN ONE COPY

Music by
J. S. FEARIS

Words by
JESSIE BROWN POUNDS

Price 50c

EUTERPEAN
QUARTETTE

HARRIET LEVINGER
FIRST SOPRANO

FANNIE LEVINGER
SECOND SOPRANO

KATHERINE BAEHRENS
SECOND ALTO.

JEANNETTE BAUHOF
FIRST ALTO.

Published by
E. O. EXCELL
FINE ARTS BUILDING. —————— MICHIGAN AVENUE.
CHICAGO

Press of Rayner, Dalheim & Co. Chicago

Beautiful Isle of Somewhere

Words by
Mrs. JESSIE BROWN POUNDS

Music by
J. S. FEARIS

Some-where the sun is shin - ing, Some-where the song - birds dwell; ___

Hush, then, thy sad re - pin - ing; God lives, and all is well. ___

REFRAIN

DEDICATED TO THE
New York Sunday World.

The BAND PLAYED ON

WORDS BY

JOHN F. PALMER.

MUSIC BY

Chas. B. Ward.

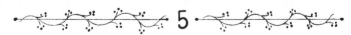

5

Published by

THE NEW-YORK MUSIC CO.,
57 WEST 28TH ST. NEW-YORK.
CHAS. SHEARD & CO LONDON, ENGL.

THE BAND PLAYED ON.

Words by
JOHN F. PALMER.

Music by
CHARLES B. WARD.

Marcia.

Allegretto.

Matt Ca sey formed a so-cial club that beat the town for style, And
Such kiss ing in the cor-ner and such whisp'-ring in the hall, And
Now when the dance was o-ver and the band played home sweet home, They

hire-d for a meet-ing place a hall _____ When
tell-ing tales of love be-hind the stairs _____ As
played a tune at Ca sey's own re-quest. _____ He

pay day came a - round each week they greased the floor with wax. And
Ca - sey was the fa - vor - ite and he that ran the ball. Of
thank'd them ver - y kind - ly for the fa vors they had shown. Then he'd

danced with noise and vig - or at the ball, _____ Each
kiss - ing and love - mak - ing did his share, _____ At
waltz once with the girl that he loved best. _____ Most

Sat - ur - day you'd see them dressed up in Sun - day clothes, Each
twelve o - clock ex - act - ly they all would fall in line, Then
all the friends are mar - ried that Ca - sey used to know, And

lad would have his sweet-heart by his side._____ When Ca-sey led the
march down to the din-ing hall and eat._____ But Ca-sey would not
Ca-sey too has tak-en him a wife._____ The blond he used to

first grand march they all would fall in line, Be-hind the man who
join them al-though ev'-ry thing was fine, But he stayed up-stairs and
waltz and glide with on the ball room floor, Is hap-py miss-is

was their joy and pride,_____ For _____
ex-er-cise his feet, _____ For _____
Ca-sey now for life, _____ For _____

CHORUS.
Valse

Ca-sey would waltz with a straw-ber-ry blonde, And the Band played

on, _____ He'd glide cross the floor with the girl he a - dor'd, and the Band

played on, _____ But his brain was so load-ed it near-ly ex-plod-ed, The

poor girl would shake with a - larm. _____ He'd ne'er leave the girl with the straw-ber-ry

curls, And the Band played on. _____

The Band Played On 19

 Nº 1 in Ab

 Nº 2 in Bb

 Nº 3 in C

BECAUSE

SONG

WORDS BY

EDWARD TESCHMACHER

MUSIC BY

GUY D'HARDELOT.

Price 60 Cents

CHAPPELL & Co. LTD
41 East Thirtyfourth Street
NEW YORK
TORONTO 347 YONGE ST.

LONDON

MELBOURNE

BECASE
SONG

Words by
EDWARD TESCHEMACHER

French words and
Music by
GUY d'HARDELOT

THE NOVELTY SONG OF THE CENTURY

BEDELIA

THE IRISH COON SONG SERENADE

Emma Carus

WORDS BY   MUSIC BY

WILLIAM JEROME   JEAN SCHWARTZ

Published by
SHAPIRO,
87-89 CLARK ST.
CHICAGO, ILL.
PHELAN BLDG.
SAN FRANCISCO CAL.
BERNSTEIN 5
AND COMPANY.
45 West 28th Street, NEW YORK.

STARMER

BEDELIA.

Words by
WILLIAM JEROME.

Music by
JEAN SCHWARTZ.

There's a charming Ir-ish la-dy with a rogu-ish win-ning
If you love me— Be-de-lia half as much as I love

way, Who has kept my heart a bump-in' and a jump-in' night and day, She's a
you, There is noth-ing in this world can ev-er cut our love in two, For I'll

flow-er from Kil - lar-ney with a Tip-per - a - ry smile, She's the best that ev - er

give you all my mon-ey on the day that we are wed, I will cook for you and

poco rit.

came from Er - in's Isle_____ And I find my-self a sing-ing all the while._____

ev - en bake the bread_____ And I'll ev - en bring your breakfast up to bed._____

CHORUS.

a tempo. mf–f

Be - de - lia,_____ I want to steal ye,_____ Be - de - lia_____ I love you

so,_____ I'll be_____ your Chauncey Ol - cott_____ If

Bill Bailey, Won't You Please ---- Come Home?

Successfully Sung by
MR. CARROLL JOHNSON

Words & Music By

Hughie Cannon

Co-Author & Composer Of

"I Hate To Get Up Early In The Morn"
"Just Because She Made Dem Goo Goo Eyes"

Published by HOWLEY, HAVILAND & DRESSER
1260 1266 Broadway. NEW YORK.
Grand Opera House Block Chicago. Chas Sheard & Co London.

Bill Bailey, Won't You Please Come Home?

Words and Music by HUGHIE CANNON.

On one sum-mer's day........
Bill drove by dat door.......

Sun was shin-ing fine,........ The la-dy love of old Bill Bail-ey was hanging clothes on de
In an au-to-mo-bile,........ A great big dia-mond, coach-and foot-man, hear dat big wench

'Mem- ber   dat   rain - y   eve   dat   I   drove   you   out,   Wid   noth - ing   but   a   fine   tooth

comb?..........   I   knows   I'se   to   blame;   well,   ain't   dat   a   shame?   Bill

1.

2.

Bai - ley,   won't   you   please   come   home?.........   home?...........

THE MOST BEAUTIFUL BALLAD EVER WRITTEN.

A BIRD IN A GILDED CAGE

SUNG WITH GREAT SUCCESS BY

May A. Bell

WORDS BY
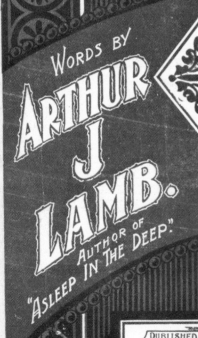
ARTHUR J LAMB.
AUTHOR OF
"ASLEEP IN THE DEEP."

MUSIC BY

HARRY VON TILZER.
COMPOSER OF
"MY OLD NEW HAMPSHIRE HOME."

PUBLISHED BY
SHAPIRO, BERNSTEIN & VON TILZER
NEW YORK.
45 WEST 28th ST
CHICAGO.
53 DEARBORN ST

A BIRD IN A GILDED CAGE.

Words by ARTHUR J. LAMB.

Music by HARRY VON TILZER.

1. The ball-room was filled with fash-ions throng, It
2. I stood in a church-yard just at eve', When

shone with a thou-sand lights,_____ And there was a wo-man who
sun - set a - dorned the west,_____ And looked at the peo-ple who'd

passed a - long, The fair - est of all the sights,_____ A
come to grieve, For loved ones now laid at rest,_____ A

girl to her lov - er then soft - ly sighed, There's rich - es at
tall mar - ble mon - u - ment marked the grave, Of one who'd been

her com - mand; ____ But she mar - ried for wealth, not for
fash - ions queen, ____ And I thought she is hap - pi - er

love he cried, Though she lives in a man - sion grand. ____
here at rest, Than to have peo - ple say when seen. ____

Allarg.

CHORUS.

She's on - ly a bird in a gild - ed cage, A beau - ti - ful

sight to see,_____ You may think she's hap - py and free from

care, She's not, though she seems to be,_____ 'Tis sad when you think of her

wast-ed life, For youth can-not mate with age,_____ And her beau-ty was

sold, For an old mans gold, She's a bird in a gild - ed cage._____

Allarg.   *sost.*

D. C.

Featured by Janet Allen the Famous Comedienne.
THE BIRD ON NELLIE'S HAT.
OR
YOU DON'T KNOW NELLIE LIKE I DO!
YOU DON'T KNOW NELLIE, LIKE I DO!
Janet Allen
WORDS BY
ARTHUR J. LAMB
MUSIC BY
ALFRED SOLMAN
authors of
"THE LINGER LONGER GIRL"
"THE HOUSE OF HITS"
Published by JOS. W. STERN & CO. 34 East 21st St. NEW YORK
MARK STERN BUILDING
NEW YORK CHICAGO AND LONDON
LONDON JOS. W. STERN & CO.
ALBERT & SON, SYDNEY, AUSTRALIAN AGENTS
50
4/-

"The Bird on Nellie's Hat."

Written by
ARTHUR J. LAMB.

Composed by
ALFRED SOLMAN.

39

was a lit - tle bird, That lit - tle bird knew lots of things, It did, up - on my word; And
pret - ty things ga - lore, But ev' - ry thing that Nel - lie said the bird had heard be - fore; And
life seemed all in vain, Un - til up - on Fifth A - ve - nue He met his Nell a - gain; Said

in it's qui - et way, It had a lot to say, As the lov - ers strolled a - long:____
as he took her hand, And said: "Oh, aint it grand!" Nel - lie wink - ed the other eye:____
he: "We meet once more!" Said she: "Love's dream is o'er! But we can be real good friends:____

p tranquillo

Refrain
a tempo

1. "I'll be your lit - tle hon - ey, I will pro - mise that!" Said
2. "Now I hav' - n't caught a fish, what do you think of that!" Said
3. "And I'll keep your pres - ents, hon - ey, just for old times' sake!" Said

a tempo

Nel - lie as she rolled her dream - y eyes.____ "It's a
Nel - lie with a most be - witch - ing look.____ "You can
Nel - lie as she rolled her dream - y eyes.____ "She has

shame to take the mon-ey!" said the bird on Nel-lie's hat, "Last
bet she knows her bus'-ness!" said the bird on Nel-lie's hat, "And
fixed him good and plen-ty!" said the bird on Nel-lie's hat, "Oh,

night she said the same to John-ny
Wil - lie is the fish she's goin' to
Wil - lie, Wil-lie, when will you be

Wise!" Then to Nel - lie Wil - lie whis-pered as they fond-ly kissed: "I'll
hook!" "Oh, it's twelve o' clock," said Wil - lie, as he took her home; "I'll
wise!" Well, but how a - bout the di - a - mond en - gage-ment ring? "Of

bet that you were nev - er kissed like that!" "Well, he don't know Nel - lie like
bet you're nev - er out as late as that!" "Well, he don't know Nel - lie like
course, said Wil - lie, you'll re - turn me that!" "Well, he don't know Nel - lie like

il basso ben marca

I do!" Said the sauc - y lit - tle bird on Nel - lie's hat.
I do!" Said the sauc - y lit - tle bird on Nel - lie's hat.
I do!" Said the sauc - y lit - tle bird on Nel - lie's hat.

sf   *p grazioso*   *f*

to

The Bird on Nellie's Hat 41

Songs from

❀ HOYT'S ❀

A Trip To Chinatown

MUSIC BY

PERCY GAUNT

NEW YORK

Published by T. B. HARMS & CO. 18 East 22nd St

LONDON:

FRANCIS, DAY & HUNTER, 195 Oxford Street.

Entered at Stationers' Hall, London, Eng.   Copyright MDCCCXCII by T. B. Harms & Co.

THE BOWERY.

Words by CHAS. H. HOYT.　　　　　　　　　　　　Music by PERCY GAUNT.

43

quiet walk; Folks who are "on to" the ci - ty say,
me he knew; Then a po - lice - man came walk - ing by,
thieves be - fore; First he sold me a pair of socks,
time at all; Just the min - ute that I sat down
nev - er stop; I, cut it short, he mis - un - der - stood,
out a - live; When the po - lice - man heard my woes,

Bet - ter by far that I took Broad - way; But I was
Chased him a - way, and I ask'd him why? "Was - n't he
Then said he, "how much for the box?" Some - one said
Girls be - gan sing - ing, "New Coon in Town," I got up
Clipp'd down my hair just as close as he could; He shaved with a
Saw my black eyes and my bat - tered nose, "You've been held

out to en - joy the sights, There was the Bow - 'ry a
pull - ing your leg," said he; Said I "He nev - er laid
"two dol - lars!" I said "three!" He emp - tied the box and gave
mad and spoke out free, "Some - bo - dy put that man
ra - zor that scratch'd like a pin, Took off my whis - kers and
up!" said the "cop - per" fly! "No, sir! but I've been knock'd

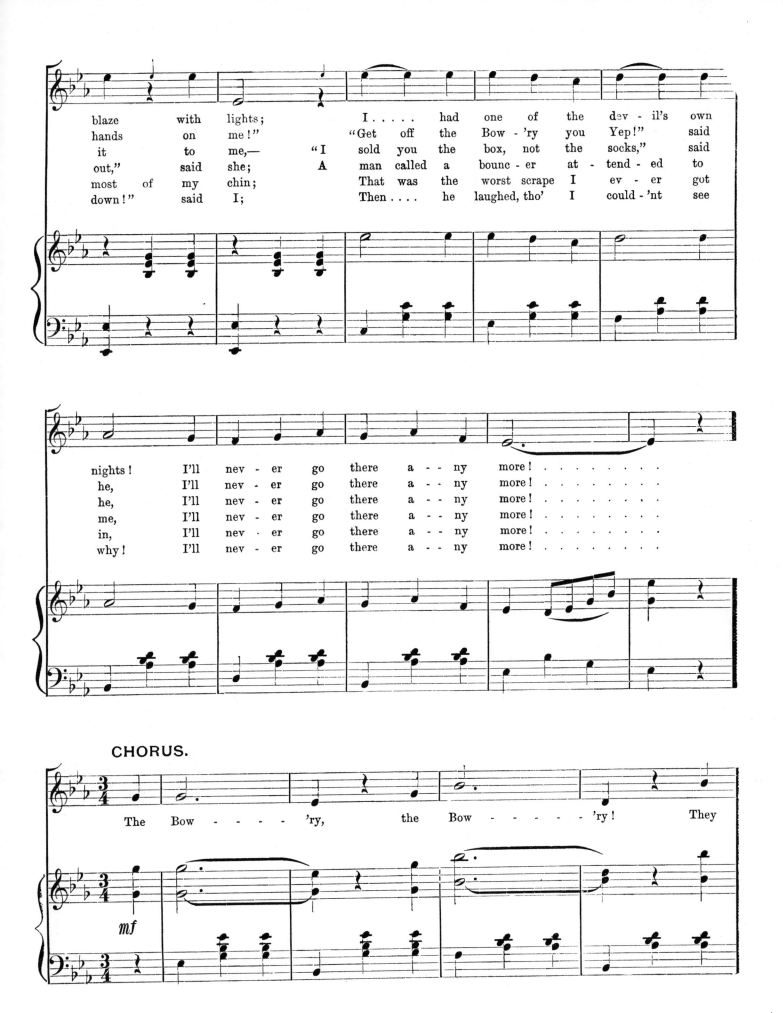

blaze with lights; I..... had one of the dev - il's own
hands on me!" "Get off the Bow - 'ry you Yep!" said
it to me,— "I sold you the box, not the socks," said
out," said she; A man called a bounc - er at - tend - ed to
most of my chin; That was the worst scrape I ev - er got
down!" said I; Then.... he laughed, tho' I could - 'nt see

nights! I'll nev - er go there a - - ny more!........
he, I'll nev - er go there a - - ny more!........
he, I'll nev - er go there a - - ny more!........
me, I'll nev - er go there a - - ny more!........
in, I'll nev - er go there a - - ny more!........
why! I'll nev - er go there a - - ny more!........

CHORUS.

The Bow - - - - 'ry, the Bow - - - - 'ry! They

mf

say   such   things, and   they   do   strange   things on   the   Bow - - - -

'ry!   The   Bow - - - 'ry!   I'll   nev - er   go   there   a - ny

D.C.

more! . . . . ,

(After last verse.)

D.C. *f*

cresc.

ff

Break the News to Mother.

Words and Music by CHAS. K. HARRIS.

Arr. by JOS. CLAUDER.

Andante.

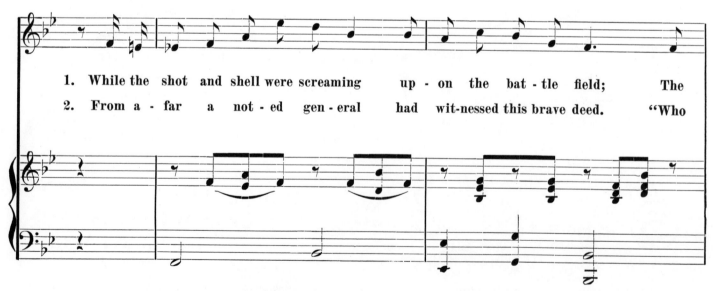

1. While the shot and shell were screaming   up - on the bat - tle field;   The
2. From a - far a not - ed gen - eral   had wit - nessed this brave deed.   "Who

boys in blue were fight - ing their no - ble flag to shield; Came a
saved our flag? speak up lads; 'twas no - ble, brave, in - deed!" There he

cry from their brave cap - tain, "Look, boys! our flag is down; Who'll
lies, sir," said the cap - tain, "he's sink - ing ver - y fast;" Then

vol - un - teer to save it from dis - grace?" "I will," a young voice shout - ed, "I'll
slow - ly turned a - way to hide a tear. The gen - eral in a mo - ment, knelt

bring it back, or die;"   Then sprang in - to the thick-est of the fray;   Saved the
down be - side the boy;   Then gave   a cry that touch'd all hearts that day.   "It's my

flag but gave his young life;   all for his coun-try's sake.   They
son, my brave, young he - ro;   I thought you safe at home."   "For-

brought him back and soft-ly heard him say:
give me, fath - er. for I ran a - way."

CHORUS.

Very slow.

Just break the news to moth - er, She knows how dear I love her, And

tell her not to wait for me, For I'm not com - ing home; Just

say there is no oth - er Can take the place of moth - er; Then

kiss her dear, sweet lips for me, And break the news to her."

rit.

D.C.

 The Song that Beats "McGinty."

"THE CAT CAME BACK"

WORDS AND MUSIC BY **HARRY S. MILLER,** AUTHOR OF

"I'm 17 To-day," "Not On Your Life, Says Dolan," "Keep Your Eye On Duffy," and his next big "hit" will be a comic song entitled
"HE'S GOT FEATHERS IN HIS HAT." (This last-named piece will be issued in August.)

PUBLISHED BY
WILL ROSSITER,
THE POPULAR SONG PUBLISHER,
MAIN OFFICES, **56** FIFTH AVE., CHICAGO. Branch, **377** Sixth Ave., New York.

"THE CAT CAME BACK."

Arr. by OTTO BONNELL.

Words and Music by HARRY S. MILLER.

Author of "I'm 17 to-day," "Not on your Life, says Dolan," etc., etc.

1. Dar was ole Mis - ter John - son, he had troub - le of his own,
2. De cat did hab some com - pa - ny one night out in de yard,

He had an ole yal - ler cat that would-n't leave its home; He tried eb - 'ry-thing he knew to
Some one frowed a boot-jack, an' dey frowed it might - y hard, Caught de cat be - hind de ear, she

HARRY VON TILZER'S
GREATEST NOVELTY HIT

GO ON AND

Coax Me

WORDS BY
ANDREW B.
STERLING

MUSIC BY
HARRY
VON TILZER

GILLETTE
SISTERS

OUR TRADE MARK

HARRY VON TILZER
MUSIC PUBLISHING CO.
37 W 28 ST NEW YORK. CHICAGO. FRISCO. LONDON

Go On And
Coax Me.

Words by
ANDREW STERLING.

Music by
HARRY VON TILZER.

Dedicated to THE MISSES ELLA AND MILLIE CANNON.
N.Y. CITY.

Comrades.

SONG

Written and Composed

BY

Felix McGlennon.

WALTZ. ③   SONG. ④ x   MARCH. ③
BY VRAI GAUTIER.   BY JAS. J. FREEMAN.

NEW YORK;
S. T. GORDON & SON. 13 EAST 14TH ST.

COMRADES.

WORDS AND MUSIC BY   FELIX M^cGLENNON.

1. We from child-hood play'd to-geth-er, My dear comrade Jack and I;— We would

2. When just bud-ding in - to manhood, I yearn'd for a sol-dier's life;— Night and

3. I en - list - ed, Jack came with me, And ups and downs we shared; For a

Tempo di Valse.

Com - rades, com - rades ev - er since we were boys;

Shar-ing each oth-er's sor - rows, sharing each oth-er's joys;

Comrades when manhood was dawn-ing, Faithful what-e'er might be-tide; When danger

threatened, my darling old comrade was there by my side! side!

1.   2.

D.S.

4. In the night, the sav-age foe-man Crept a-round us as we lay! To our arms we leap'd and faced them, Back to back we stood at bay! As I fought, a sav-age at me Aim'd his spear, like light-ning's dart, But my com-rade sprang to save me, And re-ceiv'd it in his heart! ___

Chorus D.C.

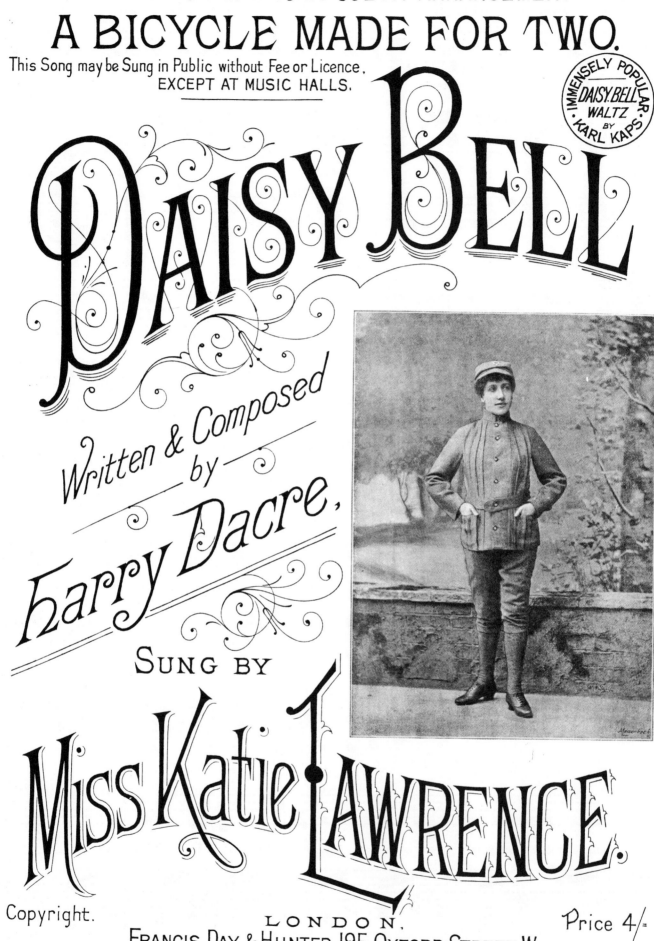

DAISY BELL.

WRITTEN AND COMPOSED   BY **HARRY DACRE.**

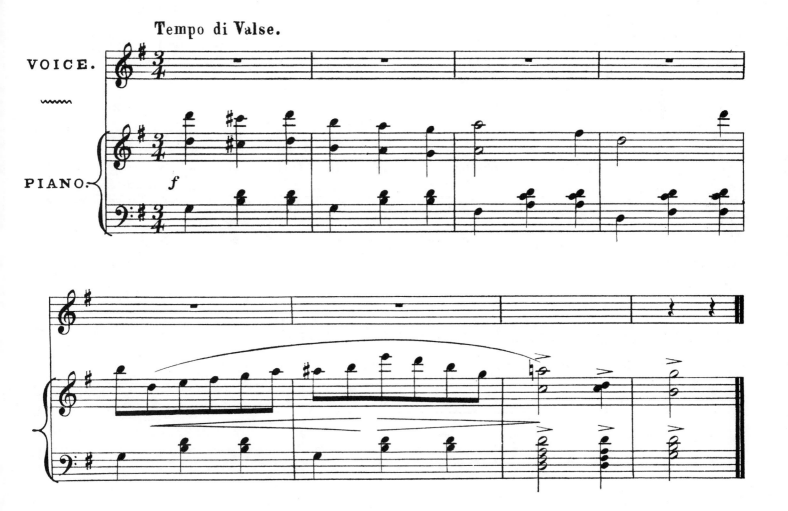

TO M.E.M.

DEAR OLD GIRL

5

WORDS BY
RICHARD HENRY BUCK

MUSIC BY
THEODORE F. MORSE

1440 BROADWAY, NEW YORK

HOWLEY, DRESSER COMPANY.

GRAND OPERA-HOUSE BLOCK, CHICAGO
ST ANN BUILDG SAN FRANCISCO
CANADIAN AMERICAN MUSIC COMPANY, TORONTO
CHAS. SHEARD & CO. LONDON

SUCCESSFULLY SUNG BY

Frank W. Shea

DEAR OLD GIRL.

WORDS BY
RICHARD HENRY BUCK.

MUSIC BY
THEODORE F. MORSE.

'Twas a sun-ny day in June, when the birds were all in tune, and the songs they sang all seemed to be of

Dark and drear the world has grown, as I wan-der all a-lone, and I hear the breez-es sob-bing thro' the

you,.......... And the words I came to speak, brought the blush-es to your cheek, as you

pines,.......... I can scarce hold back my tears, when the south-ern moon ap-pears, for 'tis

Dear Old Girl.

whis-pered "yes," and fond-ly kissed me, too............ I could see the love light shine, in your

on our hum-ble cot-tage where it shines.......... Once a-gain we seem to sit, when the

bright eye, sweet-heart mine, When the preach-er said the words that made us one,............. And you

eve-ning lamps are lit With our fac-es turned to-ward the gold-en west,............. When I

were a faith-ful wife, thro' the chang-ing scenes of life, 'Till the Mas-ter said your work on earth was done.........

prayed that you and I ne'er would have to say, 'good-bye,' But that still to-geth-er we'd be laid to rest.........

Dear Old Girl.

Sheridan & Flynn's Greatest Hit!

DOWN WENT

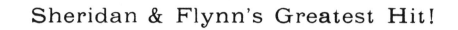

McGINTY

Dressed in His Best Suit of Clothes

COMIC SONG.

—WORDS AND MUSIC—

—BY—

JOSEPH FLYNN.

SONG, 40.   SCHOTTISCHE, 40.   WALTZ, 40.

BROOKLYN, N. Y.:

PUBLISHED BY **SPAULDING & KORNDER**, 487 FULTON ST.

Down Went McGinty.

SONG AND CHORUS.

Words and Music by JOSEPH FLYNN.

1. Sun - day morn - ing just at nine, Dan Mc - Gin - ty dress'd so fine, Stood look -
2. From the hospi - tle Mac went home, When they fix'd his bro - ken bones, To find
3. Now Mc - Gin - ty raved and swore, About his clothes he felt so sore, And an
4. Now Mc - Gin - ty thin and pale One fine day got out of jail, And with

- ing up at a ver - y high stone wall; When his friend young Pat Mc-Cann, Says, I'll
he was the fa - ther of a child; So to cel - e - brate it right, His friends
oath he took he'd kill the man or die; So he tight - ly grabb'd his stick And hit
joy to see his boy was near - ly wild; To his house he quick - ly ran To meet

CHORUS.

1st Cho. Down went McGin-ty to the bot-tom of the wall, And tho' he won the five, He was more dead than alive, Sure his
2d Cho. Down went McGin-ty to the bot-tom of the hole, Then the driv-er of the cart Give the load of coal a start, And it
3d Cho. Down went McGin-ty to the bot-tom of the jail Where his board would cost him nix, And he stay'd exact-ly six, They were
4th Cho. Down went McGin-ty to the bot-tom of the say, And he must be ver-y wet For they haven't found him yet, But they

ribs, and nose, and back were broke from getting such a fall, Dress'd in his best suit of clothes. . . .
took us half an hour to dig Mc- Gin - ty from the coal, Dress'd in his best suit of clothes. . . .
big long months he stopp'd For no one went his bail, Dress'd in his best suit of clothes. . . .
say his ghost comes round the docks Before the break of day, Dress'd in his best suit of clothes. . . .

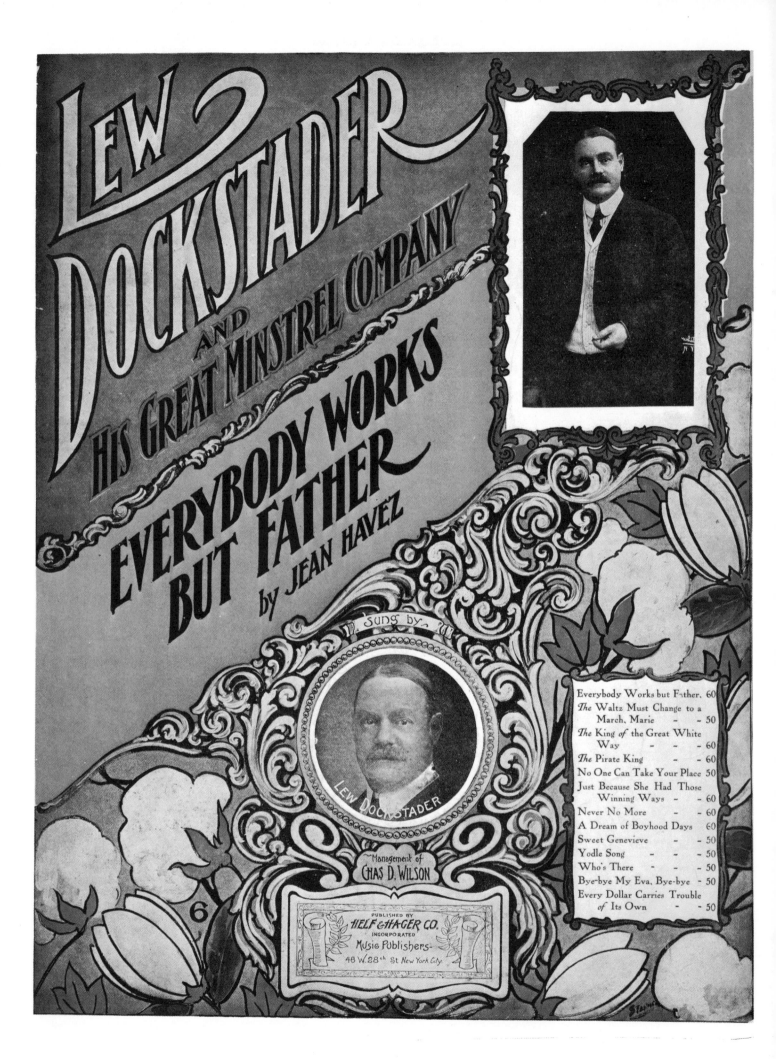

Everybody works but Father.

by JEAN HAVEZ.

Allegretto.

f

Moderato. *till ready.*

mf

VOICE.

Eve - ry morn -ing at
A man namedWork moved
At beat - ing car - -pets

six o' - clock   I go to my work,
in - to town, and fa - ther heard the news,   With
fa - ther said he sim - ply was im - mense,   We

Ov - er coat but-toned up 'round my neck   no job would I   shirk,
Work, so   near   my   fa - ther start-ed   shak-ing in his   shoes,   When
took the   par - lor   car-pet out   and   hung it   on the   fence,   My

Win - ter   wind blows 'round my   head   cut - ing   up   my   face,   I
Mis - ter   Work walked   by   my   house   he   saw with great sur - prise,   My
moth-er said: "now   beat it   dear, with   all   you   might and main,"   And

tell   you what   I'd   like to have   my   dear old   fa - ther's   place.
fa - ther sit - ting   in his chair   with   blind-ers   on   his   eyes.
fa - ther beat it   right back to   the   fire - side   a - gain.

Chorus.

Eve-ry-bod-y works but fa - ther And he sits a-round all day,

Feet in front of the fire — Smok-ing his pipe of clay,

Moth - er takes in wash - ing So does sis - ter Ann,

Eve-ry-bod-y works at our house but my old man. man.

FORTY-FIVE MINUTES FROM BROADWAY

SONG SUCCESSES FROM

GEO. M COHAN'S

LATEST MUSICAL PLAY
✦ PLAYED BY ✦
FAY TEMPLETON
UNDER THE DIRECTION OF
KLAW & ERLANGER

FORTY-FIVE MINUTES FROM ✦ BROADWAY

SONGS of the PLAY

1. RETIRING FROM THE STAGE
2. I WANT TO BE A POPULAR MILLIONAIRE
3. MARY'S A GRAND OLD NAME
4. FORTY-FIVE MINUTES FROM BROADWAY
5. STAND UP AND FIGHT LIKE HELL
6. SO LONG MARY

5

PUBLISHED BY F. A. MILLS. 48 WEST 29TH ST., NEW YORK.

"Forty-five Minutes from Broadway."

GEO. M. COHAN.

Tempo di Valse.

The West, so they say, is the home of the jay, And Mis - sou - ri's the
When the bun - co men hear that their game is so near, They'll be swarming here

state that can grind them. This may all be, but just
thick - er than bees are; In Bar - num's best days, why he

take it from me, You don't have to go out West to find them. If
nev - er saw jays, That were eas - ier to get to than these are. You

you want to see the real jay del - e - ga tion, The place where the
tell them old jokes and they laugh till they sick - en; There's gig - gles and

real ru - bens dwell, _____ Just hop on a train at the
grins here to let. _____ I told them that one a - bout

Grand Cen - tral Sta tion, Get off when they shout "New Ro - chelle." _____
"Why does a chick - en" The ru - bens are all laugh-ing yet. _____

CHORUS.

On - ly for-ty-five minutes from Broad - way, think of the changes it
On - ly for-ty-five minutes from Broad - way, not a ca - fé in the

brings; _____ For the short time it takes, what a diff'rence it makes In the
town; _____ Oh! the place is a bird, no one here ev - er heard Of Del-

ways of the peo - ple and things. _____ Oh! what a fine bunch of ru -
mon - i - co, Rec - tor or Browne. _____ With a ten dol - lar bill you're a spend -

bens, Oh! what a jay at-mos - phere; _____ They have whiskers like hay, and im-
thrift; if you o - pen a bot-tle of beer _____ You're a sport so they say, and im-

ag - ine Broadway on - ly for - ty - five minutes from here. _____ On - ly here. _____
ag - ine Broadway on - ly for - ty - five minutes from here. _____ On - ly here. _____

Popular Songs
SUNG BY
Du Rell Twin Brothers

THE FOUNTAIN IN THE PARK.   40¢   FOUNTAIN IN THE PARK SCHOTTISCHE. 40¢

NEW YORK
PUBLISHED BY
WILLIS WOODWARD & C?
842-844 BROADWAY

THE FOUNTAIN IN THE PARK.

SONG AND DANCE.

ED. HALEY.

While stroll-ing in the park one day.... All in the mer-ry month of
We ling-er'd there be-neath the trees.... Her voice was like the fra-grant

May..... A ro-guish pair of eyes they took me by sur-prise In a
breeze.... We talked of hap-py love un-til the stars a-bove When her

moment my poor heart the stole a way! . . Oh a sun_ny smile was all she gave to
lov_ing "yes" she gave my heart to please_. . Oh a sun_ny smile was all she gave to

me. . . . . And of
me. . . . .

course we were as hap_py as could be. . .
course we were as hap_py as could be. . .

So neat_ly I raised my hat. . . . . And made a po_lite re_mark. . . I

nev-er shall forget that lovely af-ternoon, When I met her at the foun-tain in the park....

DANCE.

GIVE MY REGARDS TO BROADWAY

ONE OF THE
MUSICAL HITS *from*
GEO. M. COHAN'S
LATEST PLAY

"LITTLE JOHNNY JONES"

Words &
Music by
GEO. M. COHAN

THE
YANKEE
DOODLE   COMEDIAN

F. A. MILLS
48 WEST 29TH ST.
NEW YORK

"Give My Regards To Broadway."

GEO. M. COHAN.

start for Old New York once more? _____ With
smile and charge it up to me; _____ Men-tion

tear - dimmed eye they say good - bye, they're friends with
my name ev - 'ry place you go, as 'round the

out a doubt; _____ When the man on the pier
town you roam; _____ Wish you'd call on my gal, Now re-

Shouts,"Let them clear," as the ship strikes out. _____
mem - ber, old pal, when you get back home. _____

GOOD-BYE
MY LADY LOVE

Introduced & Sung with Great Success by

IDA EMERSON.

WORDS & MUSIC BY
JOS. E. HOWARD

COMPOSER OF
"HELLO MA BABY"
"HONEY, WILL YOU MISS ME
WHEN I'M GONE" ETC.

PUBLISHED BY
CHAS. K. HARRIS
NEW YORK
CHICAGO
CANADIAN-AMERICAN MUSIC CO. LTD. TORONTO, CANADA.
WICKINS & CO. LONDON
AUSTRALIAN OFFICE, ALBERT & SON 137-139 KING ST SYDNEY

5

Good Bye, My Lady Love.

JOS. E. HOWARD.
Arr. by Al. La Rue.

So _____ you're going a -
When _____ the dew - drops

way _____ Be - cause your heart _____ has gone a - stray,
fall, _____ 'Tis then your heart, _____ I know, will call.

And _____ you promised me _____ That you would
So _____ be ware, my dove, _____ Don't trust your

CHORUS.

Good bye, my la - dy love, Fare - well, my tur - tle - dove, You are the
i - dol and dar - ling of my heart, But some day you will come
back to me, ___ And love me ten - der - ly, ___ So good bye, my
la - dy love, good bye. ___ bye. ___

VOCAL SELECTIONS
FROM

THE FORTUNE TELLER

COMIC OPERA IN 3 ACTS.

BOOK BY
HARRY B. SMITH.

MUSIC BY
VICTOR HERBERT.

AS PRODUCED BY
The Alice Nielsen Opera Co.

GIPSY LOVE SONG

50

BARITONE & MEZZO-
SOPRANO IN C.

BASS IN A.

PUBLISHED BY
M. WITMARK & SONS.

NEW YORK · SUCCESS IS WORK
CHICAGO · SUCCESS IS WORK

CHAS. SHEARD & CO. LONDON, ENG. — WHALEY ROYCE & CO. TORONTO, CAN.
COPYRIGHTED FOR GREAT BRITAIN & ALL BRITISH COLONIES & POSSESSIONS.
PARIS.   LIEPSIC.

GYPSY LOVE SONG.

(Slumber on, my little gypsy sweetheart.)

Words by Harry B. Smith.

Music by Victor Herbert.

Baritone and Mezzo Bass in A.

1. The birds of the for - est are call-ing for thee___ And the shades and the glades___ are lone - ly;___ Summer is there with her blos - soms fair,___ And you are ab - sent on - ly.___ No

2. The fawn that you tamed has a look in its eyes___ That doth say "We are too___ long part - ed;"___ Songs that are trolled by our com - rades old___ Are not now as they were___ light heart - ed.___ The

grove,_____ Can you hear me, hear me in that dreamland

Where your fan - cies rove? Slum - ber on, my

lit - tle gyp-sy sweet - heart, Wild lit-tle wood - land dove,

Can you hear the song that tells you All my heart's true love?_____

"Hearts and Flowers."
A New Flower Song.

C. Fischer's Edition.

Words by
MARY D. BRINE.

Music by
THEO. MOSES-TOBANI.

1. Out a-mongst the flow-ers sweet, Lin - gers pret - ty Mar-gue-rite,
2. When I say, "Oh Mar-gue-rite, All my heart is at your feet,

Sow-ing with her hands so white, Fu - ture blos-soms, fair and bright.
Turn it to a gar-den fair, See it blos-som 'neath your care.

Blue eyed gen - tle Mar - - gue-rite!____
For my Mar - gue - rite____ I know!

3. Blush-es deep-en in her cheek, Ere the shy red lips can speak,

"Ah! but what if weeds should grow, Mongst the flow-ers you bid me sow?"

HELLO! MA BABY.

By *HOWARD* and *EMERSON.*

Moderato.

1. I'se got a lit - tle ba - by, but she's
2. This morn - ing, thro' the 'phone, she said her

(Hel - lo! Hel - lo! Hel - lo!

out of sight, I talk to her a - cross the tel - e - phone;...... I'se
name was Bess, And now I kind of know where I am at;........ I'se

-nects me with ma hon - ey, then I rings the bell, And
oth - er coon will win her, and my game is lost, And

this is what I say to ba - by mine,............
so each day I shout a - long the line,............

CHORUS.

"Hel - lo! ma ba - by, Hel - lo! ma hon - ey,

Hel - lo! ma rag - time gal,.... ...... Send me a kiss by

HER EYES DON'T SHINE LIKE DIAMONDS.

Three Little Lads Love-story.

By DAVE MARION.

1.   Three lit - tle lads were seat - ed one day,   and their love sto - ries did
2. When Tom grew to manhood he wed a dear girl, and Frank, his old pal did the

tell, ...   Tom told of Kit - ty, who was so pret - ty, Frank
same, ...   Jack went a - way, re - turned home one day, and

told of his sweet-heart Nell. . . . . . Then the last one to speak was
with him brought fortune and fame. . . . . . . And on his dear friends one

poor lit-tle Jack, un-to his pals he did say: . . . . "I'll tell you of
night he did call, then they sat at the old fire - side; . . . . . "Are you mar-ried," Tom

one who's equalled by none," and this was his sto-ry that day. . . . .
said, but Jack shook his head, "I've a sweetheart," and then he re - plied: . . . . .

CHORUS.

"Her eyes don't shine like dia - - - - monds, she has no gold - - en

A HOT TIME IN THE OLD TOWN.

MARCH.

SCHOTTISCHE

BY
THEO. A. METZ.

NEW YORK.

WILLIS, WOODWARD & CO.,

842 BROADWAY.

A Hot Time in the Old Town.

Words by JOE HAYDEN.

Music by THEO. A. METZ.

Moderato.

Come a-long get you read-y wear your bran, bran new gown, For dere's
There'll be girls for ev-'ry bo-dy in that good, good old town, For dere's

gwine to be a meet-ing in that good, good old town, Where you
Miss Con-so-la Da-vis an dere's Miss Gondo-lia Brown; And dere's

know-ded ev-'ry bo-dy, and dey all know-ded you, And you've
Miss Jo-han-na Beas-ly she am dressed all in red, I just

got a rab-bits foot to keep a-way de hoo-do;
hugged her and I kissed her and to me than she said:

When you hear that the preach-ing does be-gin,
Please oh, please, oh, do not let me fall,

Bend down low for to drive a - way your sin and when you
You're all mine and I love you best of all, and you must

gets re - lig - ion, You want to shout and sing, there'll be a
be my man, Or I'll have no man at all, there'll be a

hot time in the old town to - night, my ba - by.
hot time in the old town to - night, my ba - by.

CHORUS.

When you hear dem a bells go ding, ling ling, All join 'round And sweet-ly you must sing, and when the verse am through, In the cho-rus all join in, there'll be a hot time in the old town to - night.........

Ida! Sweet as Apple Cider.

Words by
EDDIE LEONARD

Music by
EDDIE MUNSON.

1 In the re – gion where the ros – es al – ways bloom,_____
2 When the moon comes steal – ing up be – hind the hill,_____

Breath – ing out up – on the air their sweet per – fume,_____
Ev – 'ry-thing a – round me seems so calm and stile,_____

Lives a dus-ky maid I long to call my own,_____
Save the gen-tle call-ing of the Whip-poor Will,_____

For, I know my love for her will nev-er die;_____
Then I long to hold her lit-tle hand in mine;_____

When the sun am sin-kin' in dat gold-en West,_____
Thro' the trees the winds are sigh-ing soft and low,_____

Ida! Sweet as Apple Cider 123

Lit - tle Rob - in Red Breast gone to seek their nests, _____
Seem to come and whis - per that your love is true, _____

Then I sneak down to dat place I love the best, _____
Come and be my own now, Sweet-heart do! oh do! _____

Ev - 'ry ev'n - ing there a - lone I sigh. _____
Then my life will seem al - most di - vine. _____

Seems tho' _____ can't live with - out you, _____

Lis - ten _____ Oh! Hon - ey do! _____

I - da! _____ I I _ do - lize yer, _____ I

love you I _ da, deed I do. _____

D.S.

I Don't Care

SONG

Words by
JEAN LENOX

Music by
HARRY O. SUTTON

EVA TANGUAY'S
Novel Song Success

5

JEROME H. REMICK & CO. New York · Detroit

I Don't Care.

Words by JEAN LENOX.

Music by HARRY O. SUTTON.

Copyright 1905 by Shapiro, Remick & Co.

My star is on the as-cen-dant, That's why I don't care.
spi-rit there is no op-press-ing, Just 'cos I don't care.

CHORUS. *Faster.*

1. I don't care,_____ I don't care,_____
2. I don't care,_____ I don't care,_____

What they may think of me,_____ I'm
If peo-ple don't like me,_____ I'll

hap-py go luck-y, Men say I am pluck-y, So
try to out-live it, I know I'll for-give it, And

jol - ly   and   care   free,_____   I don't care__
live con - ten - ted   ly,_____   I don't care__

I don't care,____   If   I   do   get   the mean and
I don't care,____   If peo - ple   do   not try to

Slow.

sto - ny stare,   If   I'm nev - er suc - cess-ful, It   won't be dis - tress-ful, 'Cos
treat me fair,   There is naught can a - maze me, Dis - like can not   daze me, 'Cos

1   **2**

I   don't   care.   care._____
I   don't   care.   care._____

Extra Verses.

3.

If I call on a friend and she's not "in,"
    Why I don't care,
I simply discover I need some pins,
    'Cos I don't care;
Her feeble slight does but amuse me,
Nothing like it could confuse me,
To hand it back none could induce me,
    Just 'cos I don't care.

Chorus.

I don't care- I don't care,
If she did mean to snub,
I'm feeling so jolly 'twould be simple folly
To even feel the "rub"
I don't care- I don't care,
If I do call on her and she's not there;
If she can't say "Hello" she's not a good fellow,
    And I don't care.

4.

They say my hair's in silly style,
    But I don't care,
They but amuse me all the while,
    'Cos I don't care;
You see my hair with me's a fixture,
And it's color's not a mixture,
When they call me living picture,
    Surely I don't care.

Chorus.

I don't care- I don't care,
If my hair is not dressed swell;
I've got no kick coming- it's vastly becoming,
And suits my face so well;
I don't care- I don't care,
I know that style like mine is mighty rare,
So no one can "Phase" me by calling me "Crazy,"
    Cos I don't care.

5.

This is the time for politics,
    But I don't care,
The winning man each party picks,
    But I don't care;
O'er new recruits each is effusive,
For that chair is Oh! so elusive,
But one can win, that is conclusive,
    That's why I don't care.

Chorus.

I don't care- I don't care,
Which of the two does win,
There's Ted whose's a wonder, and ne'er makes a blunder,
I know he won't begin;
I don't care- I don't care,
There's no doubt that they're a mighty even pair,
Either Parker or Teddy we'll welcome when ready,
    And I don't care.

6.

Judge Parker's friends say he will win,
    But I don't care,
But Teddy's friends say he is "in,"
    And I don't care,
But if Teddy is elected,
One good man is being rejected,
Parker's sure to be respected,
    That's why I don't care.

Chorus.

I don't care- I don't care,
Who gets majority,
He'll be mighty lucky- I know he'll be plucky,
And happy ought to be,
I don't care- I don't care,
Who gets into the Presidential chair,
Each one will be loyal, and treat us "right royal,"
    So I don't care.

7.

The trusts they say are doomed to die,
    But I don't care,
To crush them out young Hearst will try,
    And I don't care,
He thinks the Journal rules the nation,
That he has been our sole salvation,
Has he bumps of imagination?
    Surely I don't care.

Chorus.

I don't care- I don't care,
If folks say he has 'em bad,
He went out for glory- its quite a sad story,
He came back "to the bad,"
I don't care- I don't care,
If what I'm saying makes the dear boy swear,
His hopes were many- his chances- not any,
    But I don't care.

8.

Kuroki is a wiry Jap,
    But I don't care,
For Russians he don't give a snap,
    And I don't care,
He's small- but he knows fighting science,
In him Japan does place reliance,
In Russia's face he flings defiance,
    That's why I don't care.

Chorus.

I don't care- I don't care,
How much amunition's used,
The Czar's hopes are fleeting- his army depleting,
And Nick feels so abused,
I don't care- I don't care,
How much he tells the little Jap "Beware!"
Ever since the beginning, they've kept right on winning,
    So I don't care.

To
THE LADIES OF THE CHARITY CIRCLE,
La Porte, Ind.

I Don't Want to
Play in Your Yard

WORDS BY

PHILIP WINGATE

4

MUSIC BY

H. W. PETRIE

PUBLISHED BY

PETRIE MUSIC COMPANY,

4627 Champlain Avenue,

CHICAGO, ILL

I DON'T WANT TO PLAY IN YOUR YARD.

Words by PHILIP WINGATE.

Music by H. W. PETRIE.

1. Once there lived side by side, two lit-tle maids, Used to dress just a-like,
2. Next day two lit-tle maids each oth-er miss, Quar-rels are soon made up;

hair down in braids,..... Blue ging-'am pin-a-fores, stock-ings of red,
sealed with a kiss,....... Then hand in hand a-gain, hap-py they go,

CHAS. DILLINGHAM'S PRODUCTION

OF

Mlle. Modiste

AS·SUNG
BY··THE
FRITZI
SCHEFF
COMIC
OPERA
COMPANY

MUSIC BY
VICTOR HERBERT
BOOK & LYRICS BY
HENRY BLOSSOM

Fritzi Scheff

THEATRICAL AND MUSIC HALL RIGHTS OF THIS SONG ARE RESERVED.
FOR PERMISSION, APPLY TO THE PUBLISHERS.

M. WITMARK & SONS
NEW YORK   CHICAGO   LONDON   SAN FRANCISCO

If I Were On The Stage.

(Kiss Me Again.)

Fifi.

Lyric by
HENRY BLOSSOM.

Music by
VICTOR HERBERT.

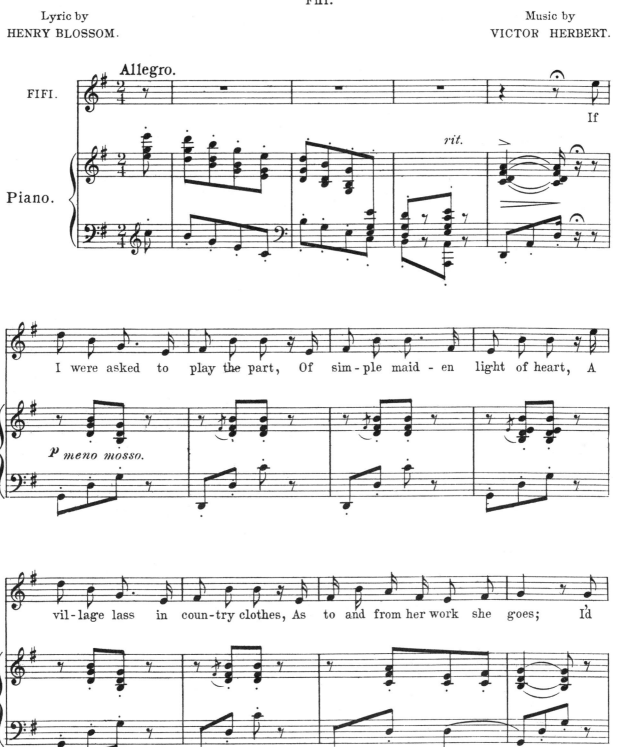

I were asked to play the part, Of sim-ple maid - en light of heart, A
vil-lage lass in coun-try clothes, As to and from her work she goes; I'd

state - ly queen with pow-dered hair, Her cost - ly gowns and jew - els rare; I

would not act the part a - miss, I'd sing a pol - o - naise like

Tempo di Polonaise. *con bravura.*

this. Ah, you will all a - gree that hap-py I should be, Ah!__

I'm queen of all the land. Ah!_____ Ah!_____

I Love You Truly

from
Seven Songs

As unpretentious as the
Wild Rose

Carrie Jacobs-Bond

Published at
THE BOND SHOP
BY
CARRIE JACOBS-BOND & SON
INCORPORATED
746 SO. MICHIGAN AVE.
CHICAGO

THE FREDERICK HARRIS CO.
Authorized Agents for the British Empire
49 QUEEN STREET EAST,   89 NEWMAN STREET WEST,
TORONTO, CANADA   LONDON, ENGLAND

PRICE 60 CENTS

2|—Net

★ High
Low

I Love You Truly

Words and Music by
CARRIE JACOBS-BOND

Andante con amore

p

I love you tru - ly, tru - ly, dear, Life with its sor - row, life with its tear, Fades in - to dreams when I feel you are near, For I love you tru - ly, tru - ly, dear.

"In My Merry Oldsmobile"

Words by
VINCENT BRYAN.

Music by
GUS EDWARDS.

Tempo di Valse.

Young John - nie Steele has an Olds - mo - bile, He loves a
They love to spark in the dark old park, As they go

dear lit - tle girl, _____ She is the queen of his gas ma -
fly - ing a - long, _____ She says she knows why the mo - tor

chine, She has his heart in a whirl. _____ Now,
goes; The spark - er's aw - ful - ly strong. _____ Each

when they go for a spin, you know, She tries to
day they spoon to the en - gine's tune, Their hon - ey -

learn the au - to, so He lets her steer while he
moon will hap - pen soon, He'll win Lu - cile with his

gets her ear, And whis - pers soft and low; Come a -
Olds - mo - bile And then he'll fond - ly croon; Come a -

ritard.

CHORUS.

way with me Lu - cile____ In my mer - ry Olds - mo -

p - f

bile, _____ Down the road of life we'll fly Au-to-mo-bubb-ling you and I. To the church we'll swift-ly steal, _____ Then our wed-ding bells will peal, _____ You can go as far as you like with me, In my mer-ry Olds-mo-bile. Come a- bile. _____

IN THE BAGGAGE-COACH AHEAD

SONG AND REFRAIN

Sweet Voiced Contralto,
IMOGENE COMER,
Queen of Descriptive Vocalists.

THE EMPIRE STATE EXPRESS OF THE NEW YORK CENTRAL.·····FASTEST TRAIN IN THE WORLD.

WRITTEN & COMPOSED BY

GUSSIE L. DAVIS.

COMPOSER OF *"IF THEY WRITE THAT I'M FORGIVEN, I'LL GO HOME." "THE FATAL WEDDING."* ETC. ETC. ETC.

Published by

HOWLEY, HAVILAND & CO.
4 East 20th Street,
NEW YORK.

5

In the Baggage Coach Ahead.
SONG and REFRAIN.

Moderato espressivo.

Words and Music by GUSSIE L. DAVIS.

1. On a dark storm-y night, as the train rat-tled on, all the pas-sen-gers had gone to bed, ... Ex-cept one young man with a babe in his arms who sat there with a bowed-down head, ... The in-no-cent

2. Ev-'ry eye filled with tears, when his sto-ry he told, of a wife who was faith-ful and true, ... He told how he'd saved all his earn-ings for years, just to build up a home for two, ... How, when Heaven had

one be - gan cry - ing just then,   As though its poor heart would
sent them this sweet lit - tle babe,   Their young hap - py lives were

break, ...   One an - gry man said, "Make that child stop its noise, for its
blessed, ...   His heart seemed to break when he mentioned her name, and in

keep - ing all of us a - wake," ....   "Put it out" said an - oth - er, "Don't
tears tried to tell them the rest, ...   Ev - 'ry wo - man a - rose to as -

keep it in here, We've paid for our berths and want rest," .....   But
- sist with the child, There were moth - ers and wives on that train, ...   And

nev - er a word said the man with the child, As he fon-dled it close to his
soon was the lit - tle one sleep-ing in peace, With no tho't of sor-row or

breast, ... "Where is its moth-er go take it to her," this a
pain, ... Next morn at a sta-tion, he bade all good-bye, "God

la - dy then soft - ly said, ... "I wish that I could" was the
bless you," he soft - ly said, ... Each one had a sto-ry to

man's sad re - ply, "But she's dead, in the coach a - head." . . . . .
tell in their home, Of the bag - gage coach a - head." . . . . .

REFRAIN.

While the train rolled on - ward, A hus - band sat in tears, ...

Think - ing of the hap-pi - ness, Of just a few short years, . . . For

ba - by's face brings pict - ures of A cher - ished hope that's dead, ... But

ba - by's cries can't wak - en her, In the bag-gage coach a - head. . . . .

In the baggage coach ahead. 4—5.

156 *In the Baggage Coach Ahead*

IN THE
GOOD OLD SUMMER TIME

Waltz Song

Words by REN SHIELDS

Music by GEORGE EVANS
"THE HONEY BOY."

5

Song	50c.
Mandolin and Guitar	40c.
Mandolin and Piano	40c.
Banjo and Guitar	40c.
Banjo and Piano	40c.
2 Mandolins and Guitar	50c.
Orchestra 10 parts and Piano	75c.
Orchestra, 14 parts and Piano	95c.
2 Mandolins, Guitar and Piano	60c.
Mixed Quartette	25c.
Male Quartette	25c.
Mandolin Solo	30c.
Banjo Solo	30c.

PUBLISHED BY
Howley, Haviland & Dresser
1260-1266 Broadway
NEW YORK
GRAND OPERA HOUSE BLOCK CHICAGO, KING'S BUILDING LONDON

IN THE GOOD OLD SUMMER TIME.

Words by Ren Shields.

Music by George Evans.

Tempo di Valse.

mf

mp

There's a time in each year that we al-ways hold dear, Good old

To swim in the pool, you'd play "hooky" from school, Good old

sum - mer time; _____ With the birds and the trees-es and

sum - mer time; _____ You'd play "ring - a - ros - ie" with

sweet scented breezes, Good old sum - mer time, _____ When your
Jim, Kate and Jos-ie, Good old sum - mer time, _____ Those

days work is ov - er then you are in clov- er, and life is one
days full of pleas-ure we now fond-ly treas-ure, when we nev-er

beau - ti - ful rhyme, _____ No trou-ble an - noy-ing, each
thought it a crime, _____ To go steal-ing cher-ries, with

one is en - joy-ing, The good old sum - mer time. _____
face brown as ber - ries, Good old sum - mer time. _____

CHORUS.

In the good old sum-mer time, _____ In the good old sum-mer time, _____

Stroll-ing thro' the sha - dy lanes, With your ba - by mine; _____ You

hold her hand and she holds yours And thats a ve-ry good sign _____ That she's your

toot-sey wootsey in The good old sum-mer time. _____ In the time. _____

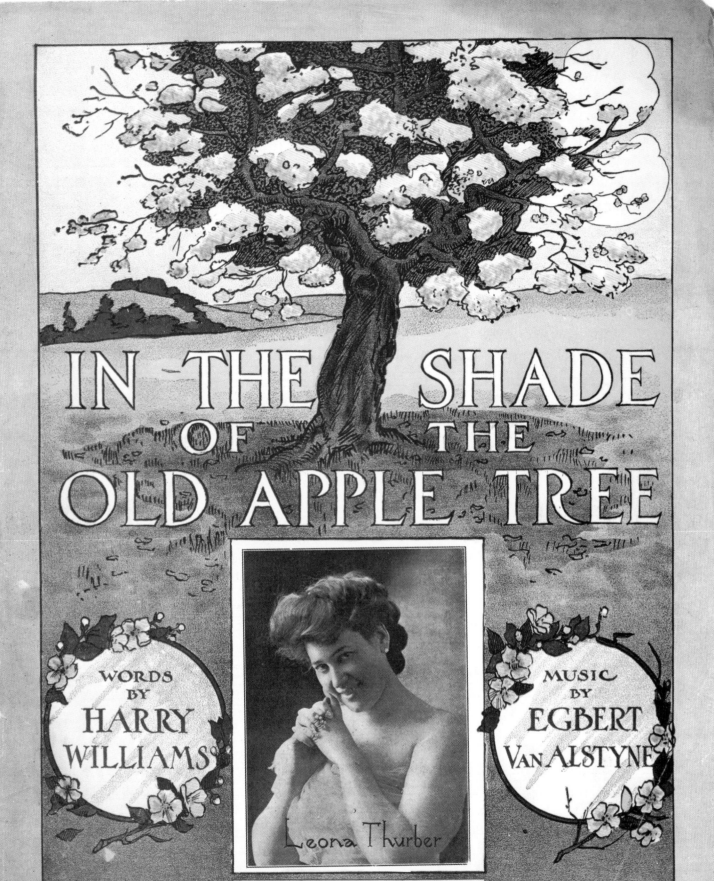

In the Shade of the Old Apple Tree.

Words by
HARRY H. WILLIAMS.

Music by
EGBERT VAN ALSTYNE.

1. The o - ri - ole with joy was sweet - ly sing - ing,____ The
2. I've real - ly come a long way from the cit - y,____ And

lit - tle brook was bab' - ling it's tune,__ The vil - lage bells at noon were gai - ly
though my heart is break-ing I'll be brave,__ I've brought this bunch of flow'rs I think they're

ring - ing____ The world seem'd bright-er than a har - vest moon;____ For
pret - ty____ To place up - on a fresh - ly mould - ed grave;____ If

Andante.

poco rit.

VOICE.

there with - in my arms I gent - ly pressed you, And
you will show me, fa - ther, where she's ly - ing, Or

blush - ing red, you slow - ly turned a - way, I
if it's far just point it out to me, Said

can't for - get the way I once ca - ressed you; I
he "she told us all when she was dy - ing, To

on - ly pray we'll meet an - oth - er day.
bur - y her be - neath the ap - ple tree."

CHORUS. *Valse lento.*

In the shade of the old ap-ple tree,_____ Where the love in your eyes I could see,_____ When the voice that I heard, like the song of the bird, Seem'd to whis-per sweet mu-sic to me;_____ I could hear the dull buzz of the bee,_____ In the blos-soms as you said to me,_____ With a heart that is true, I'll be wait-ing for you, In the shade of the old ap-ple tree._____

"In the shade of the old apple tree"

CHORUS.
Male Quartette.

Arr. by THEO. WESTMAN.

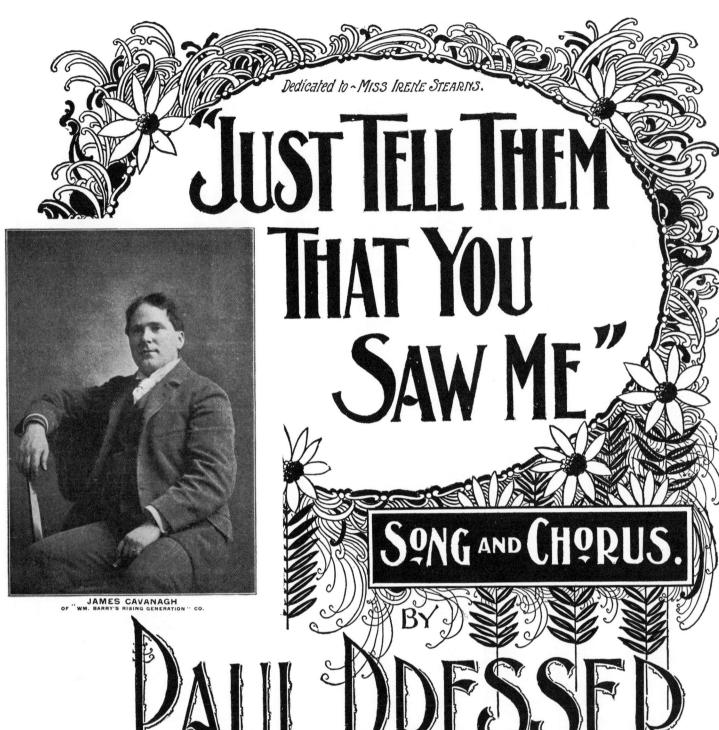

Dedicated to ~ Miss Irene Stearns.

"Just Tell Them That You Saw Me"

JAMES CAVANAGH
OF "WM. BARRY'S RISING GENERATION" CO.

Song and Chorus.

BY

PAUL DRESSER.

Author of

"The Pardon Came Too Late" ~ "Take A Seat Old Lady."
"Rosie.. Sweet Rosabel." ~ The Letter That Never Came. Etc.

TRANSCRIPTION - - 60   ④   WALTZ - - 40
Arranged by JOHN FRANCIS GILDER   By THEO. MORSE

PUBLISHED BY
HOWLEY, HAVILAND & CO.
4 East Twentieth Street, New York

JUST TELL THEM THAT YOU SAW ME.

SONG and CHORUS.

Words and Music by PAUL DRESSER,

1. While stroll-ing down the street one eve up-on mere pleasure bent, 'Twas
2. "Your cheeks are pale, your face is thin, come tell me were you ill, When

af-ter busi-ness wor-ries of the day.... I saw a girl who shrank from me in
last we met your eye shone clear and bright... Come home with me when I go Madge, the

CHORUS.

"Just tell them that you saw me, She said, they'll know the rest, Just

tell them I was look-ing well you know,... Just whis-per if you get a chance to

moth-er dear, and say,— I love her as I did long, long a - go."...

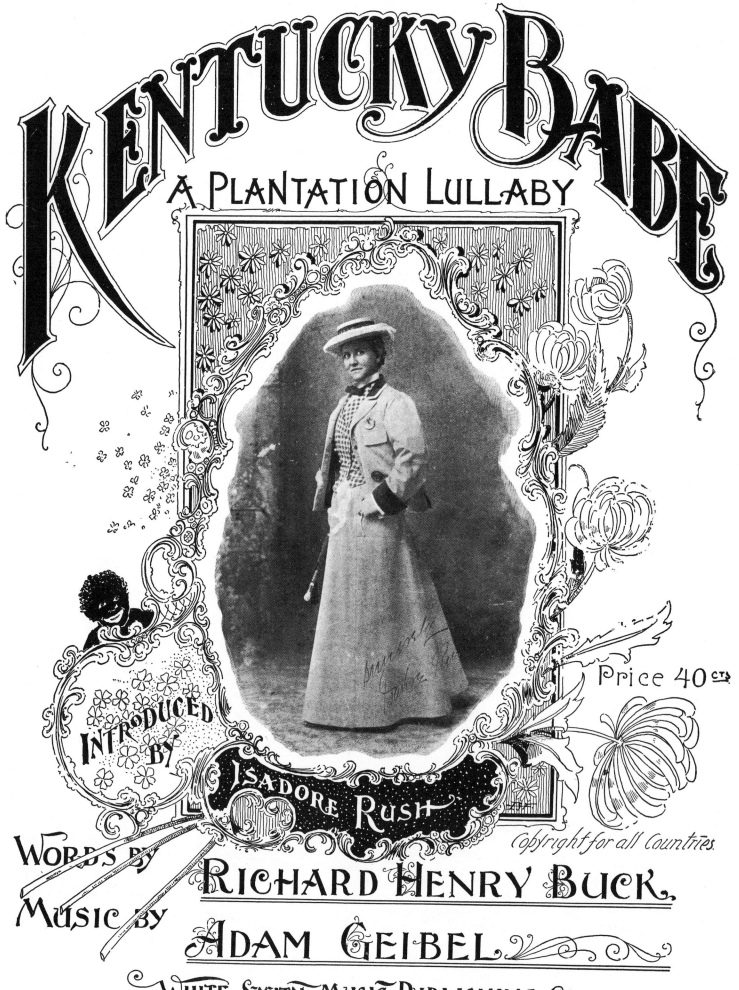

KENTUCKY BABE.

SONG AND CHORUS.

Words by RICHARD HENRY BUCK.

Music by ADAM GEIBEL.

Tempo di Schottische.

1. 'Skeet-ers am a hum-min' on de hon-ey suck-le vine, Sleep, Ken-tuck-y
2. Dad-dy's in the cane-brake wid his lit-tle dog and gun, Sleep, Ken-tuck-y

Babe! Sand-man am a com-in' to dis lit-tle coon of mine,
Babe! Pos-som, fo' yo' break-fast when yo' sleep-in' time is done,

Sleep, Ken-tuck-y   Babe!   Sil - v'ry moon am shin-in' in   de
Sleep, Ken-tuck-y   Babe!   Bo - gie man 'll ketch yo' sure un-

heah-ens up a - bove,   Bob - o - link am pin - in' fo'   his   lit - tle la - dy love,
less yo' close yo eyes,   Wait-in' jes' out side de doo' to   take yo' by sur-prise,

_p_

You is mighty luck-y,   Babe of old Ken-tuck-y,   Close yo' eyes in   sleep.—
Bes' be keepin' sha-dy,   Lit-tle colored la - dy,   Close yo' eyes in   sleep.—

cresc.   rit.

_pp_

cresc.   rit.

CHORUS.

a tempo   mf

Fly____ a - way.   fly a-way Kentucky Babe, fly a-way to rest,

a tempo mf

Fly____ a - way, Lay yo'kinky, woolly head on yo'mammy's breast.

(Humming.)

Um_____ Um_____ close yo' eyes in sleep.____

(Banjo lullaby whistle *8va* or hum ad lib.)

THE LATEST CRAZE.

LITTLE
ANNIE ROONEY.

SONG AND CHORUS.

WRITTEN, COMPOSED AND SUNG BY

MICHAEL NOLAN.

→ 40 ←

NEW YORK:
HITCHCOCK'S MUSIC STORES,
385 SIXTH AVENUE,
11 PARK ROW,   283 SIXTH AVENUE,
294 GRAND STREET.

Chicago, Ill. : NATIONAL MUSIC CO., 215 Wabash Avenue.

LITTLE ANNIE ROONEY.

Written, Composed and Sung by MICHAEL NOLAN.

1. A win-ning way, a pleas-ant smile, Dress'd so neat but quite in style,
2. The par-lor's small, but neat and clean, And set with taste so sel-dom seen, And
3. We've been en-gaged close on a year, The hap-py time is draw-ing near, I'll

Mer-ry chaff your time to wile, Has lit-tle An-nie Roon - - - ey.
you can bet, the house-hold queen, Is lit-tle An-nie Roon - - - ey. The
wed the one I love so dear, Lit-tle An-nie Roon - - - ey. My

Ev' - ry eve - ning, rain or shine, I make a call twixt eight and nine, On
fire burns cheer - ful - ly and bright, As a fami - ly cir - cle round each night, We
friends de - clare I'm in a jest, Un - til the time comes will not rest, But

her who short - ly will be mine,.... Lit - tle An - nie Roon - - - ey.
form, and ev' - ry one's de - light Is lit - tle An - nie Roon - - - ey.
one who knows its val - ue best, Is lit - tle An - nie Roon - - - ey.

CHORUS.

p, 2nd time, ff

She's my sweet - - heart, I'm her beau ;....... She's

p

my An - nie,...... I'm her Joe,......... Soon we'll

1508

LOVE'S OLD SWEET SONG.

WORDS BY

G. CLIFTON BINGHAM.

MUSIC BY

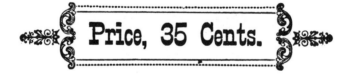

J. L. MOLLOY.

Price, 35 Cents.

NEW YORK:
PUBLISHED BY
RICHARD A. SAALFIELD,
41 UNION SQUARE,
S. W. Cor. 17th Street.

LOVE'S OLD SWEET SONG.

Words by G. Clifton Bingham.

Music by J. L. Molloy.

Once in the dear dead days beyond recall, When on the world the mists be-gan to fall,

Out of the dreams that rose in hap-py throng Low to our hearts Love sung an old sweet song;

THE MAN THAT BROKE THE BANK AT MONTE CARLO

Comic Song

Written and Composed by

FRED. GILBERT.

Pr 40¢

New York,
T. B. HARMS & C.º 18 EAST 22ND STREET.
London,
FRANCIS, DAY & HUNTER, 195 OXFORD STREET.

Copyright 1891 by Francis, Day & Hunter.

PUBLISHERS OF SMALLWOOD'S CELEBRATED PIANO METHOD.

THE MAN WHO BROKE THE BANK AT MONTE CARLO.

Sung by Charles Coborn.

Written & Composed by

FRED GILBERT.

1. I've just got here, through Pa - ris, from the sun - ny south - ern shore; I to
2. I stay in-doors till af - ter lunch and then my dai - ly walk to the
3. I pat - ron-ized the ta - bles at the Mon - te Car - lo hell Till they

MARY'S A GRAND OLD NAME

SONG SUCCESSES FROM

GEO. M COHAN'S

LATEST MUSICAL PLAY
PLAYED BY
FAY TEMPLETON
VNDER THE DIRECTION OF
KLAW & ERLANGER

FORTY-FIVE MINUTES FROM BROADWAY

SONGS of the PLAY

1. RETIRING FROM THE STAGE
2. I WANT TO BE A POPULAR MILLIONAIRE
3. MARY'S A GRAND OLD NAME
4. FORTY-FIVE MINUTES FROM BROADWAY
5. STAND UP AND FIGHT LIKE HELL
6. SO LONG MARY

5

PUBLISHED BY F. A. MILLS. 48 WEST 29TH ST., NEW YORK.

"Mary's A Grand Old Name."

GEO. M. COHAN.

My moth-er's name was Ma - ry, she was so good and
Now, when her name is Ma - ry, there is no false-ness

true; _____ Be - cause her name was Ma - ry,
there; _____ When to Ma - rie she'll va - ry,

she called me Ma - ry, too. ___ She was - n't gay or
she'll sure - ly bleach her hair. ___ Though Ma - ry's or - di -

air - y, but plain as she could be; ___
na - ry, Ma - rie is fair to see; ___

I hate to meet a fair - y who calls her-self Ma - rie. ___
Don't ev - er fear sweet Ma - ry, be-ware of sweet Ma - rie. ___

CHORUS Slowly

For it is Ma - ry, Ma - ry, plain as a - ny name can

p - f

GUS WILLIAMS

MEET ME IN St. LOUIS LOUIS

5

WORDS BY
ANDREW·B·
STERLING

MUSIC BY
KERRY
MILLS·

Also Sung With Great Success by

Will H. Sloan
Nat Wills
Lottie Gilson
Paul Barnes
Lizzie B. Raymond
Nora Bayes
Fields & Ward
Billie Clifford
Stuart Barnes
Bonnie Thornton
Evans & St. John
Vera King

F·A·MILLS 48 W. 29 St. N.Y.

Meet Me In St. Louis, Louis.*

Words by
ANDREW B. STERLING.

Music by
KERRY MILLS.

When Lou-is came home to the flat,_____ He hung up his
The dress-es that hung in the hall,_____ Were gone, she had

coat and his hat,_____ He gazed all a-round, but no
tak-en them all,_____ She took all his rings and the

wif-ey he found, So he said "where can Flos-sie be at?"_____ A
rest of his things; The pic-ture he missed from the wall._____ "What!

*In every instance "Louis" is pronounced "Louie."

Copyright 1904 by F. A. Mills, 48 West 29th St; New York.

note on the ta-ble he spied,_____ He read it just
mov-ing!"the jan-i-tor said,_____ "Your rent is paid

once, then he cried._____ It ran, "Lou-is dear, it's too
three months a - head."_____ "What good is the flat?" said poor

slow for me here, So I think I will go for a ride!"_____
Lou-is,"Read that." And the jan-i-tor smiled as he read._____

CHORUS.

"Meet me in St. Lou-is, Lou-is, Meet me at the

p-f

MIGHTY LAK' A ROSE

Words by

FRANK L. STANTON

Music by

Ethelbert Nevin.

HIGH VOICE.　　　　　　　LOW VOICE.

The John Church Company
Cincinnati. Chicago. New York.
Leipsic. London.

④
NET

To Mrs. Adele Laeis Baldwin.

Mighty lak' a rose.

(High Voice.)

Text by FRANK L. STANTON.

Music by ETHELBERT NEVIN.

Sweetest li'-l' fel-ler, Ev-'ry-bod-y knows; Dun-no what to call him, But he

might-y lak' a rose! Look-in' at his Mammy Wid eyes so shin-y blue, Mek' you think that heav'n Is

com-in' clost ter you! W'en he's dar a-sleep-in', In his li'l' place, Think I see de an-gels

cantando.

THE MOTH AND THE FLAME.

Words by *GEORGE TAGGART.*

Music by *MAX S. WITT.*

1. At a gay re-cep-tion giv-en in a man-sion grand and old, A
2. The maid-en did not un-der-stand the fa-ble that he told, A

young man met the girl he used to know; .... And
church was soon ar-rayed in ho-ly state, ... A

once a-gain the sto-ry of his hon-est love he told, The
cou-ple at the al-tar stood be-fore the crowd of guests, When a

love he'd cher-ished since long years a-go.......... But she
wo-man scream'd, "Stop! ere it is too late."........ The

sighed and sad-ly mur-mur'd that her child-hood love was past, That
vll-lain turn'd and saw his wife and rude-ly struck her down, De-

soon an-oth-er man she was to wed....... The
nounc-ing her as an im-pos-ter bold;..... But the

lov - er knew the oth - er man al - read - y had a wife. He
girl threw off the bri - dal wreath, "You cow - ard," then she cried: "My

bade fare - well, but as he went, he said; . . . .
true love warned me when this tale he told;" . . . .

CHORUS. *Andante.*

"The Moth and the Flame played a game, one day, The game of a

wo - man's heart; . . . . And the Moth that played was a

Mother Pin A Rose On Me.

Moderato.

Dave Lewis, Paul Schindler and Bob Adams.

love the coun - try air, I love the Sum - mer time, I
trav - eled all a - round, to New York for a lark, I

love to lin - ger in the shade or bask in the old sun -
went to sleep up - on a bench_____ out in Cen - tral

shine: I nev - er bor - row trou - ble, as
Park, But soon I was a - wak - ened, was

long as I eat you see, For ev - 'ry day is
fun - ny_____ don't you see, It looked like a coun - try

Sun - day, they all look a - like to me.
or - chard a pear be - neath each tree.

CHORUS.

Moth - er, moth - er, moth - er, pin a rose on me,
Moth - er, moth - er, moth - er, pin a rose on me,

p - f

Moth - er, moth - er, moth - er, pin a rose on me, It
Moth - er, moth - er, moth - er, pin a rose on me, I

does - n't mat - ter if it rains or snows, My
say old boy, —— you can plain - ly see, The

one am - bi - tion is to get the dough:
best thing for you is to twen - ty - three:

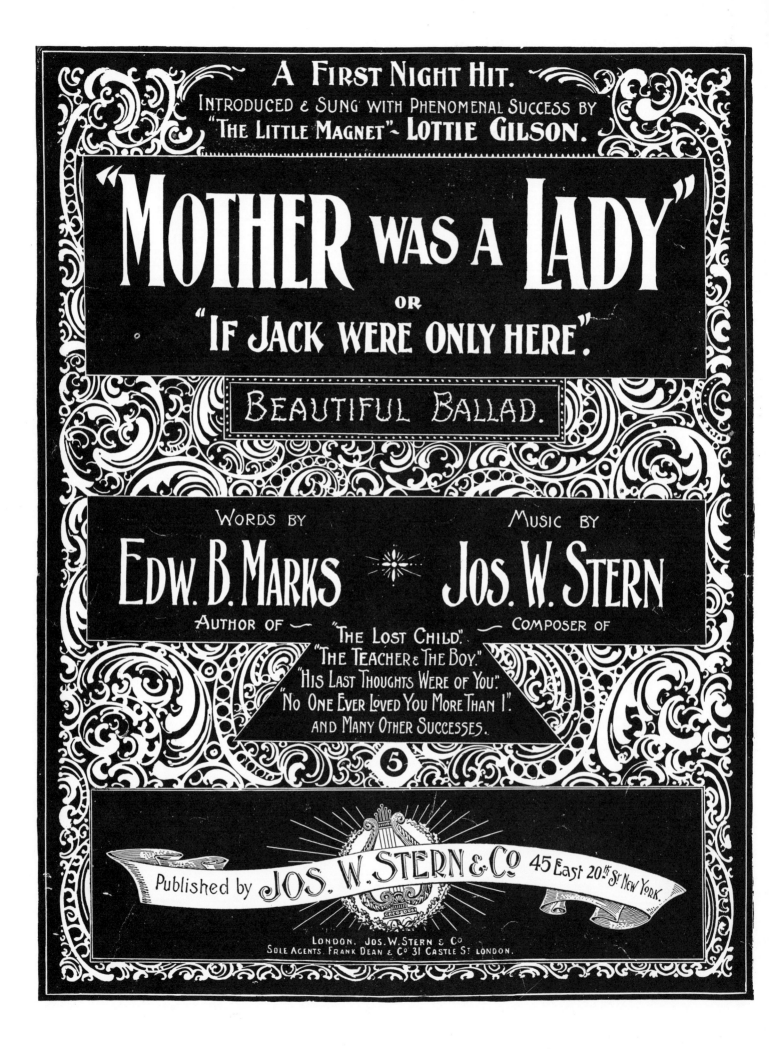

Mother Was A Lady.

or

If Jack were only here.

Words by EDW. B. MARKS.

Music by JOS. W. STERN.

Andante moderato.

1. Two drummers sat at din - ner, in a grand ho - tel one day, While
2. It's true one touch of nat - ure, it makes the whole world kin, And

din - ing they were chat - ting in a jol - ly sort of way, And
ev - ry word she ut - tered seemed to touch their hearts with - in, They

when a pret - ty wait - ress brought them a tray of food, They
sat there stunned and si - lent, un - til one cried in shame, "For -

Chorus.

Tempo di Valse.

"My mo-ther was a la-dy like yours you will al-low, And you may have a sis-ter, who needs pro-tec-tion now I've come to this great ci-ty to find a bro-ther dear And you would n't dare in-sult me Sir, If Jack were on-ly here."

My Gal Sal.

Quartette Chorus.

By PAUL DRESSER
Arranged for Quartette by
C. F. Shattuck.

They called her friv-o-lous Sal,____ A pe-cu-liar sort of a gal____ With a
heart that was mel-low, An all 'round good fel-low, Was my old pal;____ Your
troub-les sor-rows or care____ She was al-ways will-ing to share____ A
wild sort of dev-il, But dead on the lev-el, Was my gal Sal.

MY GAL SAL
or
They Called Her Frivolous Sal.

By PAUL DRESSER.

Oh, how I miss her my old pal, Oh how I'd kiss her
Gent - ly I pressed her to my breast, Soon she would take her

my gal Sal; Face not so hand - some, but
last long rest, She looked at me and

eyes don't you know That shone just as bright, as they did years a - go.
mur - mured "Pal", And soft - ly I whis - pered, "Good - bye Sal".

CHORUS. (*Slow-tenderly.*)

They called her friv-o-lous Sal,_____ A pe - cu - liar sort of a

gal, _____ With a heart that was mel - low, An all 'round good fel - low, Was

my old pal; _____ Your troubles sorrows and care, _____ She was

al - ways wil-ling to share, _____ A wild sort of dev - il, But

dead on the lev el, Was my gal Sal. _____

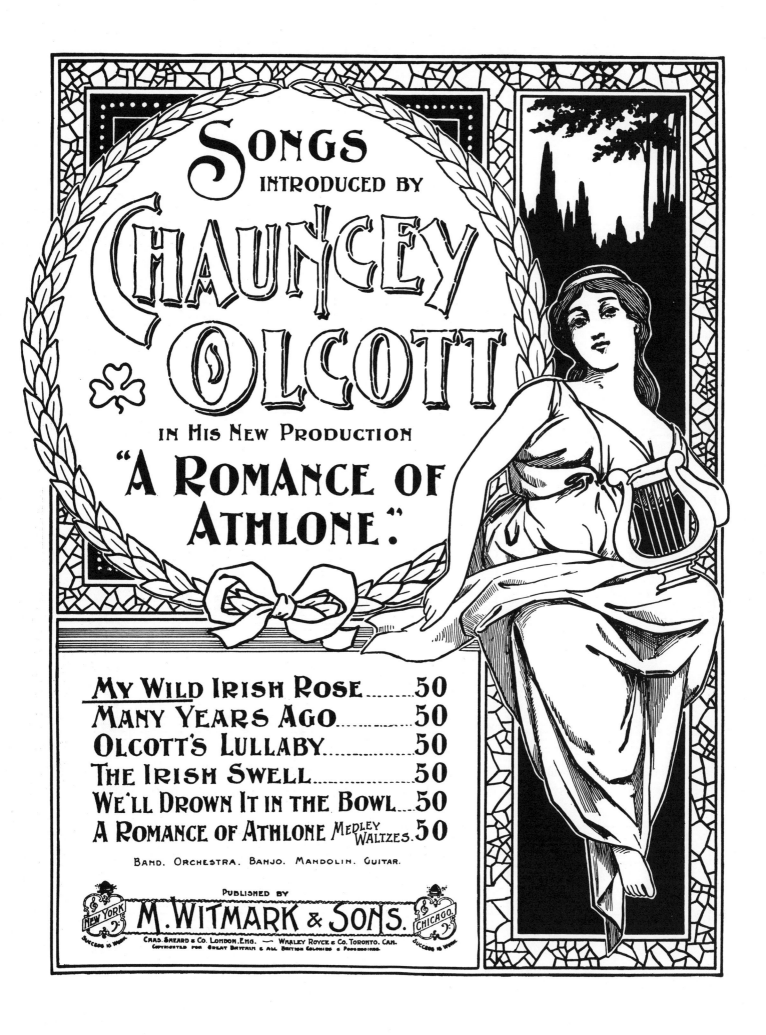

MY WILD IRISH ROSE.

Words and Music by CHAUNCEY OLCOTT.

Moderato.

1. If you lis - ten I'll sing you a sweet lit - tle song, Of a flow - er that's
2. They may sing of their ro - ses, which by oth - er names, Would smell just as

now droped and dead........ Yet dear - er to me, yes, than all of its mates, Tho'
sweet - ly, they say........ But I know that my Rose, would nev - er con - sent, To have

each holds a - loft its proud head......... 'Twas giv-en to me by a girl that I
that sweet name tak-en a - way.......... Her glan-ces are shy when e'er I pass

know, Since we've met, faith I've known no re - pose,......... She is dear - er by
by, The bow - er. where my true love grows,........ And my one wish has

far than the world's brightest star, And I call her my wild I - rish Rose.........
been that some day I may win The heart of my wild I - rish Rose.........

My wild I - rish Rose,........ the sweet-est flow'r that grows....... You may

search ev - 'ry-where, but none can com - pare, With my wild I - rish Rose......... My

wild I - rish Rose,....... The dear - est flow'r that grows, ... And some

day for my sake, she may let me take, The bloom from my wild I - rish Rose.........

As sung by Mr. Chas. E. Knorr.

Oh, promise me!

SONG

with Piano accompaniment

BY

REGINALD DE KOVEN.

Op. 50.

Sop. or Ten. in A♭   M. Sop. or Bar. in F.

Pr. 40.¢

NEW-YORK

G. SCHIRMER, 35 UNION SQUARE.

Copyright 1889 by G. Schirmer.

C

WM. A. POND & CO.,

25 UNION SQUARE, N.Y.

Oh promise me.

Words by CLEMENT SCOTT.

R. de KOVEN, Op. 50.

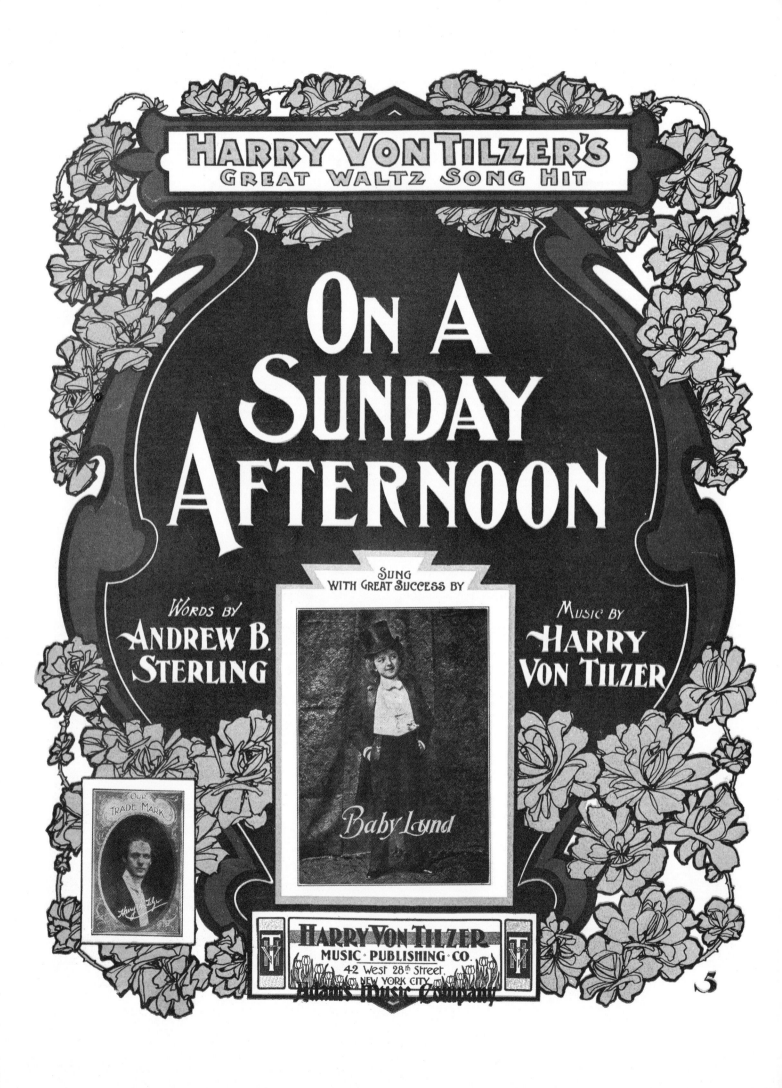

ON A SUNDAY AFTERNOON.

Words by ANDREW B. STERLING.   Music by HARRY VON TILZER.

Tempo di Valse.

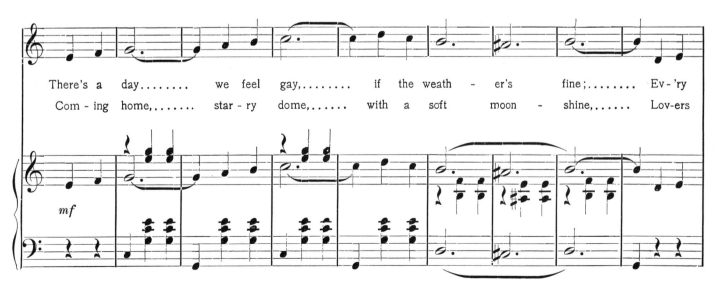

There's a day........ we feel gay,........ if the weath - er's fine;........ Ev-'ry

Com - ing home,....... star - ry dome,...... with a soft moon - shine,...... Lov-ers

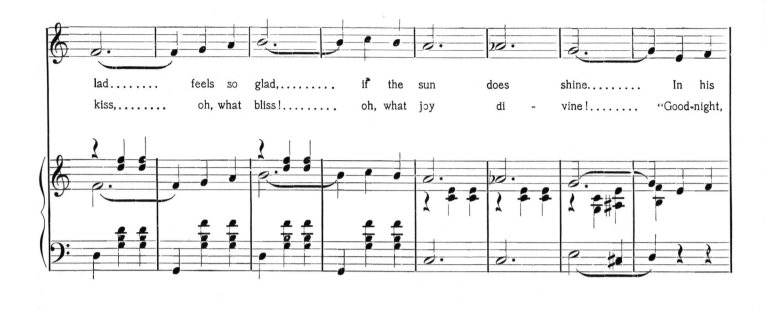

lad........ feels so glad,........ if the sun does shine........ In his
kiss,........ oh, what bliss!........ oh, what joy di - vine!........ "Good-night,

best.......... he is dressed,........ and with smil - ing face.......... He
Joe.".......... "Good-night, Flo,.......... don't for - get now, dear,........ Next

goes with his Pearl - ie, his own lit - tle girl - ie, to some nice place..........
Sun - day at two I'll be wait - ing for you on the old Iron Pier.".........

CHORUS.

On a Sun-day af-ter-noon,........ In the mer-ry month of June,........ Take a trip up the Hud-son or down the bay, Take a trol-ley to Co-ney or Rock-a-way, On a Sun-day af-ter-noon........ You can see the lov-ers spoon;........ They work hard on Mon-day, But one day that's fun day Is Sun-day af-ter-noon........ On a noon........

ON THE BANKS OF THE WABASH, FAR AWAY.

SONG and CHORUS.

Words and Music by PAUL DRESSER.

1. 'Round my Indiana homestead wave the corn-fields, In the distance loom the woodlands clear and cool, ... Oft-en

2. Many years have passed since I strolled by the river, Arm in arm, with sweetheart Mary by my side, ... It was

CHORUS.

m p Espressivo.

Oh, the moon-light's fair to-night a-long the Wa-bash, From the

fields there comes the breath of new-mown hay, ... Through the

syc-a-mores the can-dle lights are gleam-ing, On the

banks of the Wa-bash, far a-way. . . . .

D.C.

Songs of "THE OLD HOMESTEAD"

No. 1. Old Red Cradle. *Gilbert* 40.

No. 2. Rock-a-Bye Baby. *Canning* 40.

No. 3. Irene Lorraine. *W. A. Keller* 40

No. 4. "Let's make a Little Home for the Old Folks". *Wheeler.* 40.

No. 5. When Mother puts the Little Ones to Bed. " 40.

No. 6. Rock-a-Bye Baby, Waltz. *Fred Field* 40.

No. 7. " " " Galop. " " 40.

No. 8. " " " Schottische. *Fitzgibbon* 40.

No. 9. " " " Transcription. *Canning* 60.

No. 10. " " " Male Quartette. *Fred Field* 40.

No. 11. " " " Guitar or Banjo. 40.

Denman Thompson

Published by Boston Mass

Chas. D. Blake & Co. 488 Washington St

O. DITSON & CO.
BOSTON

C. H. DITSON & CO.
NEW YORK

LYON & HEALY
CHICAGO

W.ᵐ A. POND & CO
NEW YORK

JOHN CHURCH & CO.
CINCINNATI, OHIO

Copyrighted, 1887 by, Chas D. Blake & Co
Geo H Walker & Co Lith Boston

ROCK-A-BYE BABY.

SONG AND LULLABY.

Words and Music by EFFIE I. CANNING.
Author of " Tapping on the Panes," " Safely rocked in Mother's arms."

1. Ba - by is sleep - ing so co - zy and fair, While moth - er sits near in her old oak - en chair, Her
2. Grand - ma sits knit - ting close by the fire - place, With snow - y white hair and a smile on her face, The
3. Dear lit - tle ba - by, their joy and their pride, Long may he be with them what - ev - er be - tide, The

foot on the rock-er the cra-dle she swings, And though ba-by
years have passed by, yet it does not seem long, Since she rocked ba-by's
kitch-en, the cra-dle, that ten-der re-frain, In mem'-ry will

slumbers he hears what she sings.
pa-pa to sleep with that song.
lin-ger that lul-la-by strain.

LULLABY.

Rock - a-bye, ba - - by, on the tree
top, When the wind blows the cra-dle will rock, When the bough
breaks the cra-dle will fall, And down will come ba-by, cra-dle and all.

Oh — rock-a-bye, rock-a-bye, moth-er is near, Then rock-a-bye,

rock-a-bye, noth-ing to fear, For an-gels of slum-ber are hov-er-ing

near, So rock-a-bye, ba--by, moth-er is here.

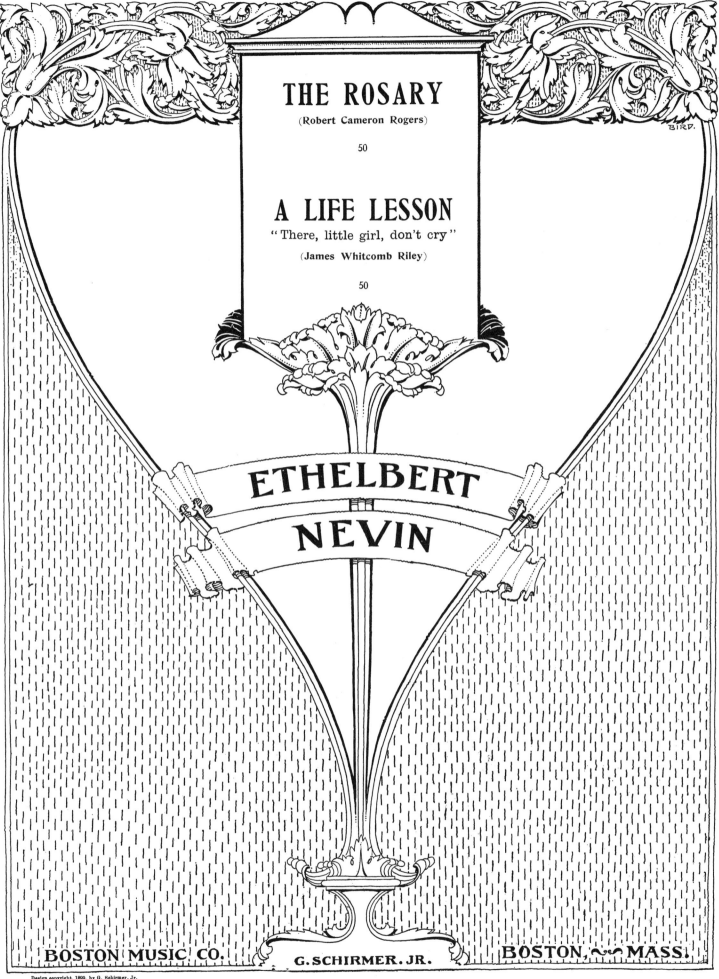

THE ROSARY
(Robert Cameron Rogers)

50

A LIFE LESSON
"There, little girl, don't cry"
(James Whitcomb Riley)

50

ETHELBERT NEVIN

BIRD.

BOSTON MUSIC CO.   G. SCHIRMER. JR.   BOSTON, ~ MASS.

The Rosary.

Text by
ROBERT CAMERON ROGERS.

Music by
ETHELBERT NEVIN.

The hours I spent with thee, dear heart,

Are as a string of pearls to me; I count them o-ver ev -'ry

one a-part, My ro - sa - ry, my ro - sa - ry.

Each hour a pearl, each pearl a pray'r, To still a heart in ab-sence

wrung: I tell each bead un-to the end, and there a

Cross is hung! O, mem-o-ries that bless and

burn!   O, barren gain and bit-ter loss!

patetico

sempre cresc.

I kiss each bead, and strive at last to learn To kiss the

f

accel.   Largo.

Cross;   sweet-heart! To kiss the Cross.

fff

A Song for the Parlor—for the Concert—or the Minstrel.

The Beautiful Ballad,

BUT NOT

Words and Music by

HARRY KENNEDY.

. . . AUTHOR OF . . .

"Molly and I and the Baby," "Empty is the Cradle," "Flower from Mother's Grave," "Hush, Don't Wake the Baby," "Old-Fashioned Photograph," "Little Empty Stockings by the Fire," etc., etc.

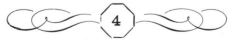

4

PUBLISHED BY

KENNEDY PUBLISHING HOUSE,

288 STATE STREET, BROOKLYN, N. Y.

AND FOR SALE AT THE FOLLOWING MUSIC STORES:

DITSON & CO.,
Broadway, New York.

T. S. KENNEDY,
Old Trafford, Manchester, Eng.

NATIONAL MUSIC CO.,
Chicago, Ill.

SAY "AU REVOIR," BUT NOT "GOOD-BYE."

Words and Music by **HARRY KENNEDY.**

1. Say "au re - voir," .... but not "good-bye," .... For parting brings ... a bit - ter
2. The wa - ters glide, ... the oars lie still, ... A rippling laugh, ... a word at

sigh; The past is gone, ... though mem-'ry gives One clinging
will: Where an - gels fear, ... fools dare to tread, Shall live for

THE BEAUTIFUL SENSATIONAL PATHETIC SONG.

SHE IS MORE TO BE PITIED THAN CENSURED.

A STORY OF LIFE'S "OTHER SIDE" TAKEN FROM AN ACTUAL OCCURRENCE.

NOTE :—

The theme of this song is indeed a delicate one to handle, and is offered in sympathy, and not defense, for the unfortunate erring creatures, the life of one of whom suggested its construction.

THE AUTHOR.

AS SUNG BY

CHAS FALKE

WORDS & MUSIC BY

5 WM. B. GRAY

AMERICA'S BEST-KNOWN & MOST SUCCESSFUL SONG WRITER. AUTHOR OF "THE VOLUNTEER ORGANIST." "OH, MISTER AUSTIN." "THE MOTHER OF THE GIRL I LOVE." "THE CHURCH ACROSS THE WAY." "WHEN YOU KNOW THE GIRL YOU LOVE LOVES YOU." & A HUNDRED OTHER HITS.

NEW YORK
PUBLISHED BY W. B. GRAY & CO 16 WEST 27TH STREET.
EUROPEAN AGENTS,
HOWARD & CO
25 GREAT MARLBOROUGH. STREET. W.
LONDON. ENGLAND.

ANY SHEET OF MUSIC YOU SEE IT ON IS GOOD.

A SYMBOL OF M

SHE IS MORE TO BE PITIED, THAN CENSURED.

PATHETIC SONG and CHORUS.

Words and Music by WM. B. GRAY.

1. At the old con-cert hall on the Bow-'ry, . .
2. There's an old fashioned church round the cor-ner, . .

'Round a ta-ble were seat-ed, one night, . . . A crowd of young
Where the neigh-bors all gath-ered one day, ... While the par-son was

fel-lows ca-rous-ing, . . . With them life seemed cheer-ful and bright, . . .
preach-ing a ser-mon, . . . O'er a soul that had just passed a-way, ...

At the ve - ry next ta - ble, was seat - ed, ... A girl who had
'Twas this same way - ward girl from the Bow - 'ry, . . . Who a life of ad-

fal - len to shame, ... All the young fel - lows jeered at her
-ven - ture had led, ... Did the cler - gy - man jeer at her

weak - ness, ... 'Till they heard an old wo - man ex - claim; . . . . .
down - fall? . . . . No, he asked for God's Mer - cy and said. . . . . . .

CHORUS.

She is more to be pit - ied than cen - sured, . . . She is more to be

helped than des - pised, ... She is on - ly a las - sie who ven - tured, . . . On

life's storm - y path, ill ad - vised, ... Do not scorn her with words fierce and

bit - ter, . . . Do not laugh at her shame and downfall, ... For a mo - ment just

rall,

stop and con - sid - er, ... That a man was the cause of it all, ...

She May Have Seen Better Days

Song

Words and Music by

James Thornton

As Sung by

W. H. WINDOM

With

Primrose & West's Minstrels

4

NEW YORK

Published by **T. B. HARMS & CO.** 18 East 22nd St

LONDON :

FRANCIS, DAY & HUNTER, 195 Oxford Street.

Copyright MDCCCXCV by T. B. Harms & Co.   English Copyright Secured.

SHE MAY HAVE SEEN BETTER DAYS.

Words & Music by James Thornton.

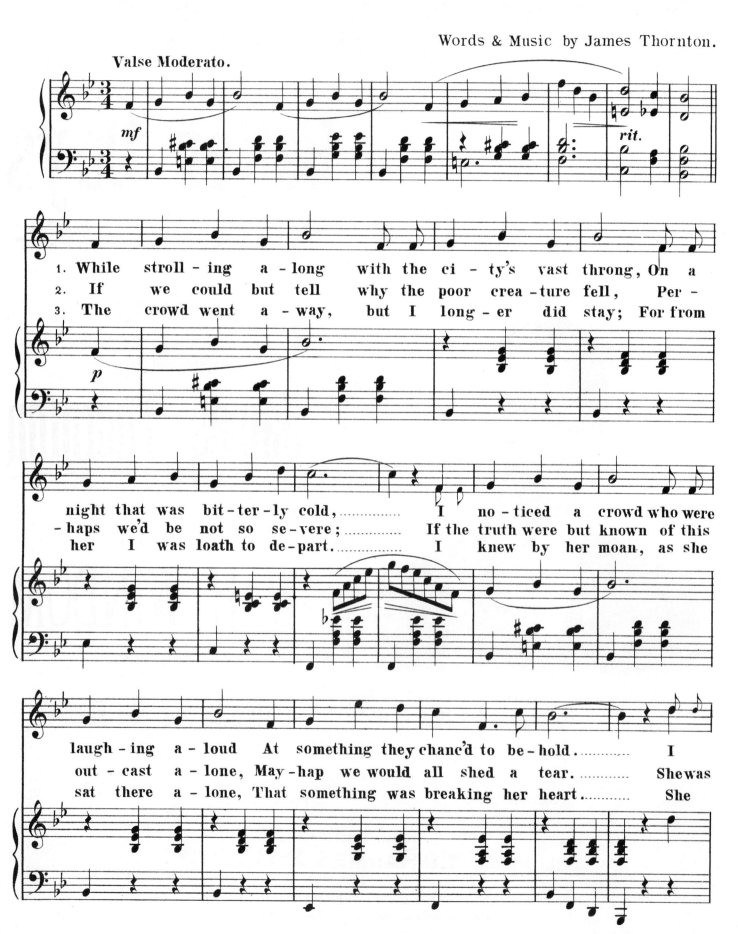

1. While stroll-ing a-long with the ci-ty's vast throng, On a
2. If we could but tell why the poor crea-ture fell, Per-
3. The crowd went a-way, but I long-er did stay; For from

night that was bit-ter-ly cold, I no-ticed a crowd who were
-haps we'd be not so se-vere; If the truth were but known of this
her I was loath to de-part. I knew by her moan, as she

laugh-ing a-loud At something they chanc'd to be-hold. I
out-cast a-lone, May-hap we would all shed a tear. She was
sat there a-lone, That something was breaking her heart. She

stopped for to see what the ob-ject could be, And there, on a
once some-one's joy, cast a-side like a toy, A-ban-doned, for-
told me her life, she was once a good wife, Re-spect-ed and

door - - step, lay............... A wom-an in tears, from the
-sa - ken, un - known........... Ev'ry man stand-ing by had a
hon - ored by all;............ Her hus-band had fled Ere

rall.

crowd's an-gry jeers — And then I heard some-bo-dy say:..........
tear in his eye, For some had a daugh-ter at home..........
they were long wed, — And tears down her cheeks sad-ly fall.........

colla voce. *rit.*

CHORUS.

She may have seen better days,......... When she was in her prime;.........

mf

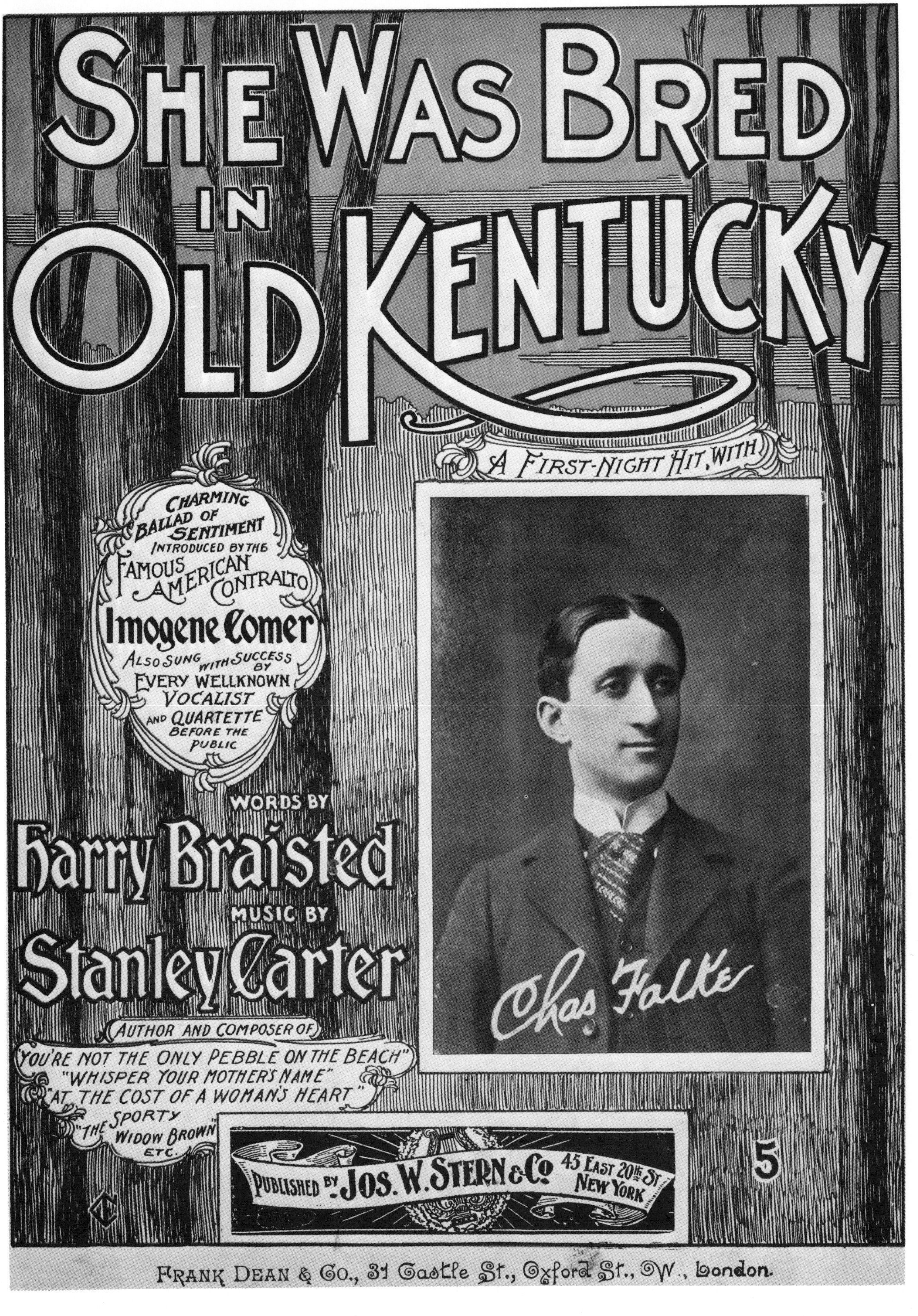

FRANK DEAN & Co., 31 Castle St., Oxford St., W., London.

SHE WAS BRED IN OLD KENTUCKY.

Words by HARRY BRAISTED.

Music by STANLEY CARTER.

Moderato.

1. When a lad, I stood one day by a cot-tage far a-way, And to me that day, all nature seem'd more
2. Man-y years have pass'd a-way since that well re-mem-ber'd day, When to that dear old Ken-tuck-y home I

grand; .... For my Sue, with blush-es red, had just promised we should wed, And I'd
came; .... And my hap-pi-ness thro' life, was my sweetheart, friend and wife, For the

come to ask her moth - er for her hand......... As I told the old, old tale, of a
sun - shine in her heart re-mained the same......... I am sit-ting all a-lone, in a

love that ne'er would fail, The grayhaired mother stroked her daughter's head,............ And I
place we've long called home, For yes-ter-day my dar-ling passed a - way;............ Tho' in

fan-cied I could trace just a tear on her kind face, As she placed my sweetheart's hand in mine and said:.........
tears, I think with joy of the day when but a boy, That I took her hand and heard her mother say:...............

CHORUS.

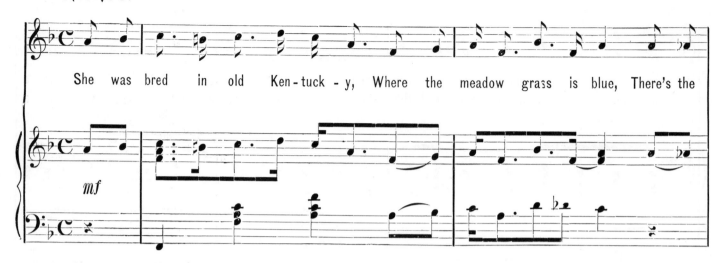

She was bred in old Ken-tuck-y, Where the meadow grass is blue, There's the

sun-shine of the country, in her face and man-ner too; She was bred in old Kentucky, Take her,

boy, you're might-y lnck-y, When you mar-ry a girl like Sue.............

Chas. B. Lawlor's Great Success

The Sidewalks
of New York

SONG AND CHORUS.

BY

CHAS. B. LAWLOR

— AND —

JAMES W. BLAKE

4

NEW YORK:

PUBLISHED BY HOWLEY, HAVILAND & CO., 4 EAST 20TH STREET.

COPYRIGHT MDCCCXCIV BY HOWLEY, HAVILAND & CO
ENGLISH COPYRIGHT SECURED.

CHARLES SHEARD & CO., 192 HIGH HOLBORN, W. C. LONDON.

THE SIDEWALKS OF NEW YORK.

SONG and CHORUS.

Arr. by CHAS. MILLER.

Words and Music by
CHAS. B. LAWLOR, and JAMES W. BLAKE.

Introduction,
Tempo di Valse.

1. Down in front of Ca - sey's, ... Old brown wood - en
2. That's where John - ny Ca - sey, ... And lit - tle Jim - my
3. Things have changed since those times, ... Some are up in

stoop, ... On a sum - mer's eve - ning, ... We
Crowe, ... With Ja - key Krause the ba - ker, ... Who
"G," . . . . . Oth - ers they are wand - 'rers. But they

Somebody's Sweetheart I Want To Be.

By COBB *and* EDWARDS.

Marcia Moderato.

1. I am so lone-ly, I am so blue, I'm hap-py on-ly when I
2. Star up a-bove me, Lis-ten to me, I have a fa-vor I would

Andrew Mack's Songs

AS SUNG BY HIM IN HIS NEW PLAY,

The Last of the Rohans

BY RAMSAY MORRIS
MANAGEMENT OF
RICH & HARRIS

THE STORY OF THE ROSE,	50¢
GRANDMOTHER'S SONGS,	50¢
JACK O'LANTERN SONG,	50¢
PAT AND HIS PIPES,	50¢
LAST OF THE ROHANS, Medley Waltz,	50c

PUBLISHED BY
HOWLEY, HAVILAND & CO
1260~66 B'WAY, NEWYORK.
MASONIC TEMPLE, CHICAGO.

THE STORY OF THE ROSE.

Words by "ALICE."

Music by ANDREW MACK.

A youth one day in a gar - den fair A rose found with-er'd and dy - - ing, And all for love, ah! love in vain, This rose was sad - ly sigh - - ing.

Heart of my heart, I love you, Life would be naught with - out you;

p

Light of my life, my darl - - ing, I love you, I love you.

rall.

a tempo.

I can for - get you nev - - er, From you I ne'er can sev - - er,

Say you'll be mine for - ev - - er: I love you..........

dim.

O sweet wild rose of a sum - mer day Thy love has all been in vain;........

Loved by a maid then cast a - way: I e - - cho thy re - frain.........

BONNIE THORNTON'S LATEST "HIT"

"THE STREETS OF CAIRO"

OR THE POOR LITTLE COUNTRY MAID

BY

JAMES THORNTON

AUTHOR AND COMPOSER OF

"MY SWEETHEART'S THE MAN
IN THE MOON"
"MY CONEY ISLAND GIRL"
"WHEN SUMMER COMES AGAIN"
— ETC. ETC.
ETC.

SONG —SCHOTTISCHE.

MDCCCXCV.

C. COPYRIGHT

~BY~ **FRANK HARDING**

ENTERED AT STATIONERS HALL LONDON ENGLAND

NEW YORK CITY

FRANK HARDINGS MUSIC HOUSE

B. FELDMAN 84 OXFORD ST. LONDON ENGLAND

FOR SALE AT ALL MUSIC STORES

STREETS OF CAIRO,

or The Poor Little Country Maid.

Arr. by G. M. ROSENBERG.

by JAMES THORNTON.

1. I will sing you a song, And it wont be ve - ry long, 'Bout a
2. She went out one night, Did this in - no - cent di - vine, With a
3. She was en - gaged As a pict - ure for to pose, To ap-

maid - en sweet, And she nev - er would do wrong,
nice young man, Who in - vit - ed her to dine,
- pear each night, In ab - bre - viat - ed clothes,

Ev - 'ry - one said she was pret - ty, She was not long in the ci - ty,
Now he's sor - ry that he met her, And he nev - er will for - get her,
All the dudes were in a flur - ry, For to catch her they did hur-ry,

All a - lone, oh, what a pit - ty, Poor lit - tle maid
In the fu - ture he'll know bet - ter, Poor lit - tle maid.
One who caught her now is sor - ry, Poor lit - tle maid.

CHORUS.

She nev - er saw the streets of Cai - ro, On the Mid - way
She nev - er saw the streets of Cai - ro, On the Mid - way
She was much fair - er far than Tril - by, Lots of more men

p 2d time *f*

she had nev-er strayed, She nev - er saw the kutch-y, kutch-y,
she had nev-er strayed, She nev - er saw the kutch-y, kutch-y,
sor - ry will be, If they dont try to keep a-way from this

Poor lit-tle coun-try maid, maid. . . . . .
Poor lit-tle coun-try maid, maid. . . . .
Poor lit-tle coun-try maid, maid. . . . . .

DAVID MONTGOMERY AND FRED. A. STONE

IN CHARLES DILLINGHAM'S PRODUCTION

The RED MILL

BOOK & LYRICS BY

HENRY BLOSSOM

MUSIC BY

VICTOR HERBERT

I'LL RING THE BELL .... .50
GOOD-A-BYE JOHN .... .50
BECAUSE YOU'RE YOU (Duet) .... A ..50
EVERY DAY IS LADIES' DAY WITH ME .... .50
WHISTLE IT (Trio) .... .50
BECAUSE YOU'RE YOU (Solo) .... .50
MIGNONETTE .... .50
YOU NEVER CAN TELL ABOUT A WOMAN .... .50
A WIDOW HAS WAYS .... .50
THE ISLE OF OUR DREAMS .... .50
THE STREETS OF NEW YORK .... .50
MOONBEAMS .... .50
THE LEGEND OF THE MILL .... .50
I WANT YOU TO MARRY ME .... .50
GO WHILE THE GOIN' IS GOOD .... .50

SELECTION .....1.00   WALTZES 75   MARCH 50
LANCIERS 50   SCORE 2.00

Theatrical and Music Hall Rights of this Song are
Reserved. For permission apply to the Publishers.

B. Wallis

M. WITMARK & SONS

NEW YORK   CHICAGO   LONDON   SAN FRANCISCO.   JOSEF WEINBERGER, LEIPZIG AND VIENNA   ALLAN & CO. MELBOURNE, AUSTRALIA   CANADIAN-AMERICAN MUSIC CO. LTD. TORONTO

The Streets of New York.

Con, Kid and Chorus.

Lyric by
HENRY BLOSSOM.

Music by.
VICTOR HERBERT.

Tempo di Valse.

Piano.

In dear old New York it's re - mark - a - ble -
If a spare af - ter - noon you should hap - pen to
What - ev - er the weath - er is - shin - ing or

ver - y! The name on the lamp-post is un - nec - ess - ar - y! You
have and you start on a lei - sur - ly stroll up Fifth Av - en - ue,
show-er - y, That does-nt "cut an - y ice" on the Bow - er - y

mere - ly have to see the girls to know what
There is where with haugh - ty air you'll see them
Eve - ry night till broad day - light, they dance and

street you're on! Fifth Av - en - ue beau - ties and
as they walk! With vel-vets and lac - es and
sing and talk! The girls are all game and they're

dear old Broad - way girls! The tail - or - made shop - pers the
sab - les en - fold - ing them, real - ly you'll near - ly fall
Jol - ly good fel - lows, They're not ver - y swell but they're

Av - en - ue "A" girls, They're strict-ly all right but they're dif - fer - ent
dead on be - hold - ing them, luck-y's the earl that can mar - ry a
none of them jeal - ous, They go it a - lone in a style of their

quite, In the diff - 'rent parts of town._____ In
girl from Fifth Av - en - ue New York._____
own On the Bow - ery in New York._____

old New York! In old New York! The peach-crop's al - ways

fine! They're sweet and fair and on the square! The

maids of Man - hat-tan for mine! You can - not see in gay Pa-

ree, in Lon-don or in Cork! The queens you'll meet on

an - y street in old New York.

Dance.

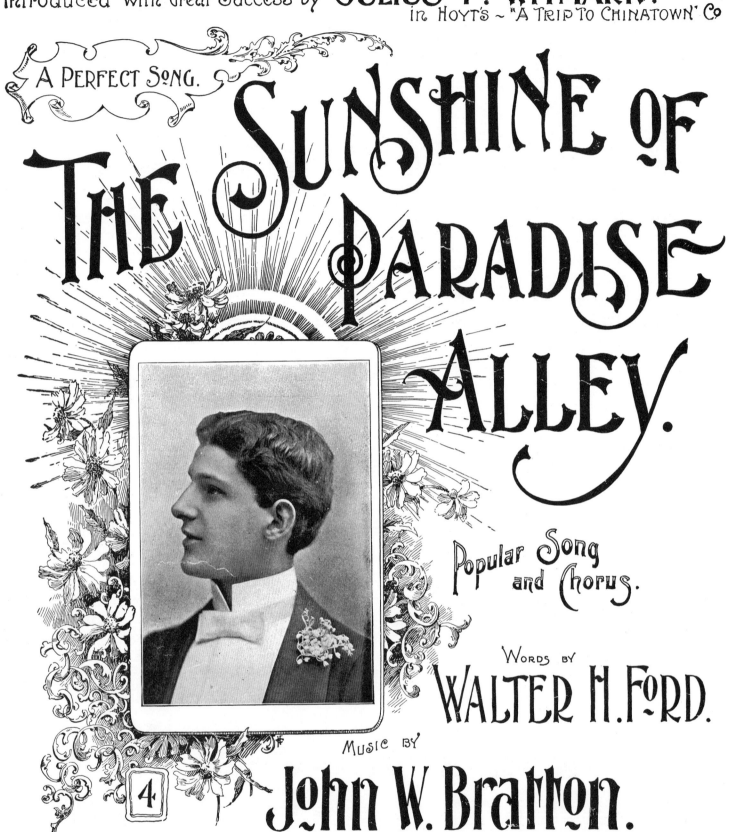

THE SUNSHINE OF PARADISE ALLEY.

SONG AND CHORUS.

Words by WALTER H. FORD.

Music by JOHN W. BRATTON.

Introduction.
Tempo di Valse.

1. There's a lit-tle side street such as of-ten you meet, Where the boys of a Sun-day night
* 2. When O'-Brien's lit-tle lad had the fev-er so bad, That no one would dare to go
3. She's had off-ers to wed by the doz-en, 'tis said, Still she al-ways re-fused them po-

ral-ly, ... Tho' it's not ve-ry wide, and it's dis-mal be-side, Yet they call the place
near him, . . . Then this dear girl so brave, said, "I think I can save, Or at least I can
lite-ly, ... But of late she's been seen with young Tom-my Kil-leen, Go-ing out for a

The second verse may be omitted at the option of the singer.

THE SWEETEST STORY EVER TOLD,

(TELL ME, DO YOU LOVE ME.)

WRITTEN FOR AND SUNG WITH GREAT SUCCESS BY MISS MYRA MIRELLA THE CHARMING VOCALIST AND SOUBRETTE.

SONG

WRITTEN AND COMPOSED BY R.M. STULTS.

AUTHOR OF "MADRIENNE" "WHEN LILIES BLOOM" -ETC-

SONG.

④

EASY TRANSCRIPTION.

BOSTON:

Published by OLIVER DITSON COMPANY. 453 to 463 Washington St.

NEW-YORK:	CHICAGO, ILL.	PHILADELPHIA:	BOSTON:
C. H. DITSON & CO.	LYON & HEALY,	J. E. DITSON & CO.	JOHN C. HAYNES & CO.
867 BROADWAY	COR. STATE & MONROE STS.	1228 CHESTNUT ST.	33 COURT & 453 WASHINGTON STS.

THE SWEETEST STORY EVER TOLD.

Mezzo Soprano or Baritone.

in F.

Words and Music by R. M. STULTS.

1. Oh an-swer me a ques-tion, love, I pray, . . My heart for thee is pin-ing day by
2. Oh tell me that your heart to me is true, . . Re-peat to me the sto-ry ev-er

day; . . . Oh an-swer me, my dear-est, an-swer true; . . . .
new; . . . Oh take my hand in yours and tell me, dear, ...

287

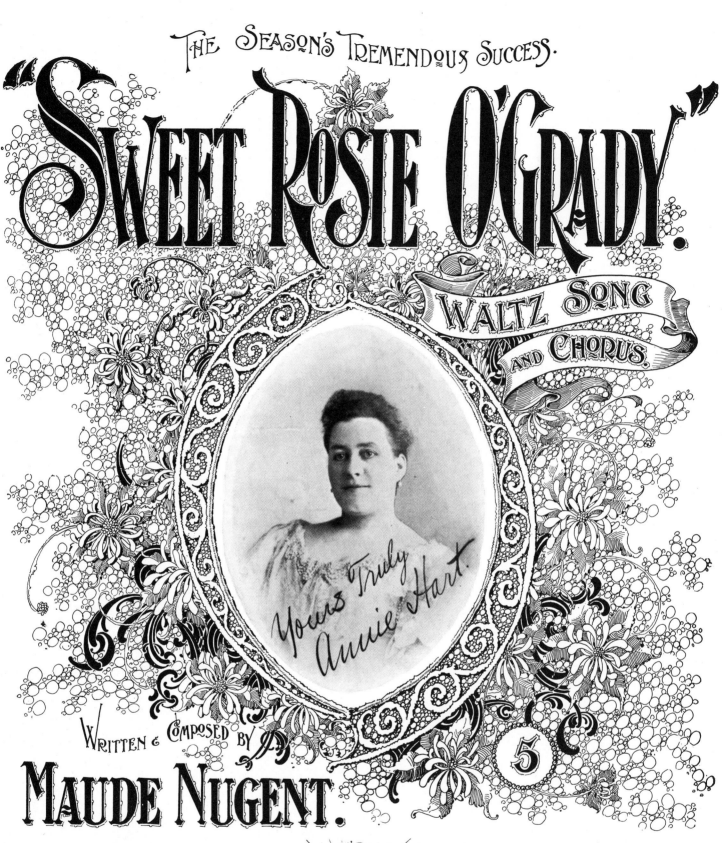

SWEET ROSIE O'GRADY.

Words and Music by Maude Nugent.

name is Rose O' Gra - dy and, I don't mind tell - ing you, That
on her fin - ger that I placed a small en - gage - ment ring, While

she's the sweet - est lit - tle Rose the gar - den ev - er grew.
in the trees, the lit - tle birds this song they seemed to sing!

CHORUS. Valse.

Sweet Ro - sie O' Gra - dy, My dear lit - tle

Rose, She's my stea - dy la - dy,

Most ev'-ry-one knows,⸺⸺ And when we are mar - ried, How hap-py we'll be;⸺⸺

I love sweet Ro - sie O' Gra - dy, And Ro - sie O' Gra - dy, loves me. me⸺⸺

TAKE BACK YOUR GOLD.

Written by Louis W. Pritzkow.

Composed by Monroe H. Rosenfeld.

1. I saw a youth and maid-en on a lone-ly ci-ty street, And
2. He drew her close un-to him and to soothe her then he tried, But

thought them lov - ers, at their meet-ing place;............... Un-
she in pride and sor - row turned a - way, ...

-til, as I drew near, I heard the girl's sad voice en - treat The
as he sought to com-fort her, she wept and soft - ly sighed, "You'll

one who heed - ed not her tear-stained face. .... "I
rue your cru - el ac - tions, Jack, some day." .... "Now,

on - ly ask you, Jack, to do your du - ty, that is all. You
lit - tle one, don't cry," he said "for though to-night we part, And

know you promised that we should be wed."................ And
though an - oth - er soon will be my bride,................ This

when he said, "You shall not want, what - ev - er may be - fall," She
gold will help you to for - get," but with a break ing heart, She

spurned the gold he of - fered her and said :................
scorned his gift and bit - ter - ly re - plied :................

CHORUS.

"Take back your gold, for gold can nev-er buy me; Take back your bribe, and promise you'll be true; Give me the love, the love that you'd de-ny me; Make me your wife, that's all I ask of you!"——

TA-RA-RA BOOM-DE-AY!

SUNG BY Miss LOTTIE COLLINS.

1. A smart and sty-ish girl you see,
2. I'm not ex-trav-a-gant-ly shy, And
3. I'm a tim-id flow'r of in-no-cence,

Belle of good so-ci-e-ty; Not too strict, but rath-er free, Yet as right as
when a nice young man is nigh, For his heart I have a try— And faint a-way with
Pa says that I have no sense—I'm one e-ter-nal big ex-pense; But men say that I'm

right can be! Nev-er for-ward, nev-er bold— Not too hot and not too cold,
tear-ful cry! When the good young man, in haste, Will sup-port me round the waist; I
just im-mense! Ere my ver-ses I con-clude, I'd like it known and un-der-stood, Tho'

But the ve-ry thing, I'm told, That in your arms you'd like to hold!
don't come to, while thus em-braced, Till of my lips he steals a taste!
free as air, I'm nev-er rude— I'm not too bad and not too good!

CHORUS.
Tempo di Marcia.

mf Ta-ra-ra Boom-de-ay! Ta-ra-ra Boom-de-ay! Ta-ra-ra Boom-de-ay!

Ta-ra-ra Boom-de-ay, Ta-ra-ra Boom-de-ay, Ta-ra-ra Boom-de-ay, Ta-ra-ra

Boom-de-ay, Ta-ra-ra Boom-de-ay!

4 You should see me out with Pa,
Prim, and most particular;
The young men say, " Ah, there you are!"
And Pa says, " That's peculiar!"
" It's like their cheek!" I say, and so
Off again with Pa I go—
He's quite satisfied—although,
When his back's turned—well, you know—
CHORUS.—Ta-ra-ra, &c.

5 When with swells I'm out to dine,
All my hunger I resign;
Taste the food, and sip the wine—
No such daintiness as mine!
But when I am all alone,
For shortcomings I atone!
No old frumps to stare like stone—
Chops and chicken on my own !
CHORUS.—Ta-ra-ra, &c.

6 Sometimes Pa says, with a frown,
" Soon you'll have to settle down—
Have to wear your wedding gown—
Be the strictest wife in town !"
Well, it must come by-and by—
When wed, to keep quiet I'll try;
But till then I shall not sigh,
I shall still go in for my—
CHORUS.—Ta-ra-ra &c.

TEASING

WORDS BY
CECIL MACK

MUSIC BY
ALBERT Von TILZER

The Two Pucks

THE YORK MUSIC CO
ALBERT Von TILZER, M'g'r.
40 WEST 28th ST., N.Y.

Teasing.

("I Was Only, Only Teasing You.")

Words by CECIL MACK.

Music by ALBERT Von TILZER.

Nev - er thought my E - va - lin - a would flirt, I'm on the a - lert 'cos my
Don't in - tend to stand her teas - ing no more, I'll go hunt - ing for gore a - round

rall. *a tempo.*

feel - ings is hurt, I caught her on the sly, A - mak - ing
some - bo - dy's door, Some - times I think I'll leave, And try to

eyes at fel - lers pass - ing by; I told her in a
find my - self an - oth - er Eve; But what's a fel - ler

gen - tle - man way, And this was all she had to say:
go - ing to do, When she rolls them eyes and says to you:

Chorus.

"Teas - ing, teas - ing, I was on - ly teas - ing you,

Teas - ing, teas - ing, just to see what you would do, (Of course you know that I was)

(Spoken or sung ad lib.)

Teas - ing, teas - ing, to find out if your love was true;

Don't be an - gry, I was on - ly, on - ly teas - ing you." —

SONGS FROM

Florodora

BOOK BY

OWEN HALL

MUSIC BY

LESLIE STUART

AS PRODUCED AT THE

NEW YORK CASINO

The Shade of the Palm - - - -	60
The Queen of the Philippine Islands (His Only Love)	60
The Fellow Who Might - - - -	60
Tact - - - - -	60
Phrenology - - - - - -	60
I Want to be a Military Man - - -	60
The Silver Star of Love - - - -	60
I've an Inkling - - - - -	60
Tell Me Pretty Maiden - - - -	60

NEW YORK,

Published by T. B. HARMS & CO. 18 East 22d St.

LONDON:

FRANCIS, DAY & HUNTER, 142, Charing Cross Road

Tell Me Pretty Maiden.

English Girls and Clerks.

By LESLIE STUART.

(GIRLS.) There are a
(MEN.) There are a

(MEN.) Tell me, pret-ty maid-en, Are there a-ny more at home like you?
(GIRLS.) Tell me, gen-tle stran-ger Are there a-ny more at home like you?

few,   kind sir,   But sim-ple girls, and pro-per too.
few,   sweet maid   And bet-ter boys you nev-er know

Then
Then

you too well   to let   you   go   And flirt with those at   home, you know,
duce them to   a girl   I in-tend   To   be   my most par - tic-u - lar friend

Well,
I

It's
It's

don't   mind,   lit - tle girl   You'll   see   I'll on - ly want   but
won't   mind,   what they do   No   man   would ev - er flirt   with

not   quite   fair to them   If   you   told them that you   were
not   worth   risk-ing it   I   know   with them you won't   a

you.
me.

I
I

must love some one, real-ly And it might as well be you!

must love some one, real-ly And it might as well be you!

THE HIT OF "FLORODORA"

TELL ME PRETTY MAIDEN

DANCE

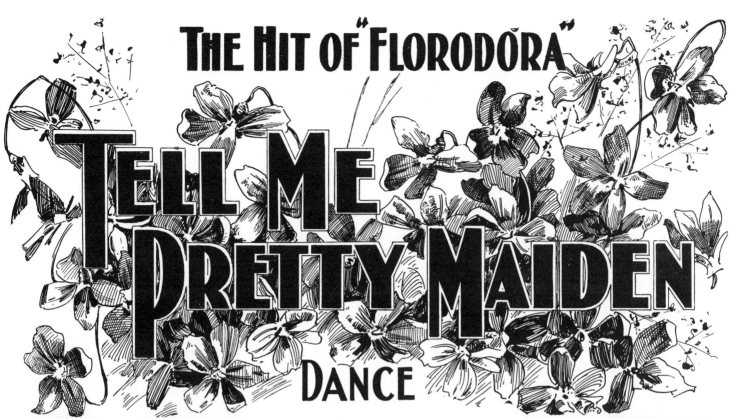

BY

LESLIE STUART

Arranged by

MAX DREYFUS

6

NEW · YORK
Published by T. B. HARMS & C.O 18 East 22nd St.
London. Eng. FRANCIS. DAY & HUNTER
142 Charing Cross Road. w.c

Those Wedding Bells Shall Not Ring Out!

Words and Music by MONROE H. ROSENFELD,
Author of
"THE SONG OF THE STEEPLE." "WITH ALL HER FAULTS
I LOVE HER STILL." AND MANY POPULAR WORKS.

1. A sex - ton stood one Sab - bath eve with -
2. The min - is - ter was speech - less and the

in a bel - fry grand,.............. A - wait - ing sig - nal from the
bride - groom stood a - mazed,.............. The con - gre - ga - tion spell - bound

church with bell - rope in his hand;............... As in the house of
sat and thought the man was crazed,............. The bride had not a

wor - ship stood a young and hap - py pair............... To pledge their
word to say, but sim - ply hung her head............. "Who is this

troth for - ev - er - more each oth - er's love to share............... The
man?" the preacher asked, "I know him not," she said................ "Then

ho - ly man then spake these words:"Be - fore you're joined for life................ Has
ring the bells," the bride - groom cried—the man knelt to en - treat—............ The

Chorus.

After first and second verses ff.   After third verse pp.

1. "Those wed - ding bells must not ring out, She is an - oth - er's bride, I
2. "Those wed - ding bells shall not ring out, I swear it on my life! For
3. "Those wed - ding bells shall not ring out, I swear it on my life! For

saw her at the al - tar-rail, We stood there side by side; She can - not claim an - oth - er's hand—She
we were wed-ded years a - go And she is still my wife! She shall not break her vows to me—She's
we were wed-ded years a - go And she is still my wife! She shall not break her vows to me—She's

dare not break the law's command—A guilt y wife you see her stand! Those bells shall not ring out."
mine through all e - ter - ni - ty—She's mine till death shall set her free–Those bells shall not ring out!"
mine through all e - ter - ni - ty—She's mine till death shall set her free–Those bells shall not ring out!"

forms lay cold with-in the aisle, the hus-band and the bride,............ As

once in life he claim'd they stood in wed-lock, side by side;.............. His

vow was kept, the bells had ceased, and with his dy-ing breath,........... These

Chorus, D. C. al 𝄐

words once more he mur-mur'd ere his lips were closed in death:..............

Chorus, D. C. al 𝄐

MAGGIE CLINE'S LATEST

COMIC SONG AND CHORUS.

THROW HIM DOWN McCLOSKEY.

WORDS AND MUSIC BY J. W. KELLEY.

COPYRIGHTED AND PUBLISHED BY HARDING BROTHERS.

HARDING'S MUSIC OFFICE

NEW YORK CITY.

"THROW HIM DOWN M'CLOSKEY."

(M'CLOSKEY'S GREAT FIGHT.)

Song & Chorus.

Words and Music by J. W. KELLY.

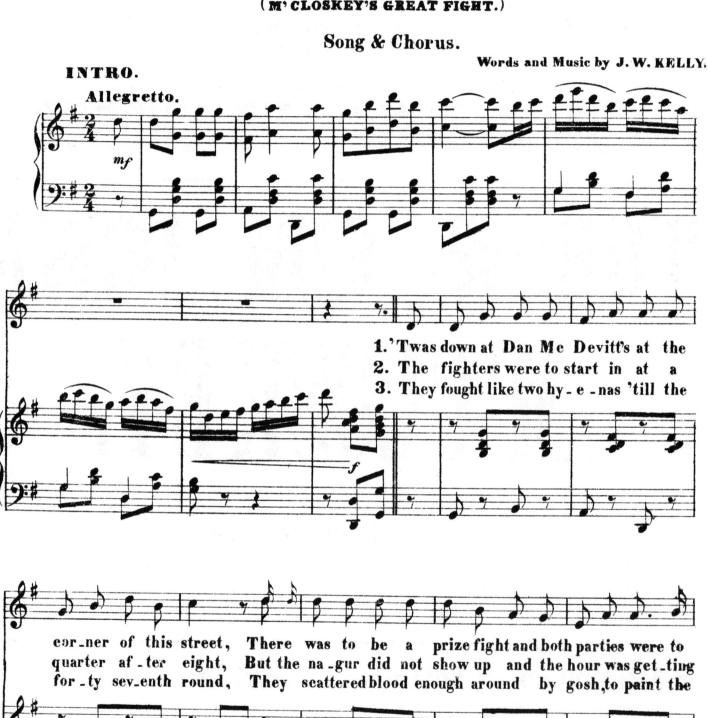

1.'Twas down at Dan Mc Devitt's at the corner of this street, There was to be a prize fight and both parties were to

2. The fighters were to start in at a quarter af-ter eight, But the na-gur did not show up and the hour was get-ting

3. They fought like two hy-e-nas 'till the for-ty sev-enth round, They scattered blood enough around by gosh, to paint the

meet; To make all the arrangements and see ev-'ry-thing was right, Mc
late; He sent a-round a mes-sen-ger who then went on to say, That the
town, Mc Closkey got a mouthful of poor Mc Crackens jowl. Mc

Closkey and a na-gur were to have a fin-ish fight; The rules were London
I _ rish crowd would jump him and he couldn't get fair play; Then up steps Pete Mc
Cracken hollered 'murthur'and his seconds hollered "foul"! The friends of both the

Prize Ring and Mc Closkey said he'd try, To bate the na-gur wid one punch or
Cracken, And said that he would fight. Stand up or rough and tum-ble if Mc
fighters that in-stant did be-gin, To fight and ate each oth-er the whole

in the ring he'd die; The odds were on Mc Closkey tho the bet_ting it was
Closkey did n't bite? Mc Closkey says I'll go you, then the sec_onds got in
par_ty start_ed in, You couldn't tell the dif_'rence in « « fighters if you'd

small, 'Twas on Mc Closkey ten to one, On the na_gur, none at all.............
place, And the fighters started in to dec _ o - rate each oth_ers face.............
try, Mc Cracken lost his up - per lip, Mc Closkey lost an eye.............

CHORUS.

"Throw him down Mc Closkey,"was to be the bat - tle cry,...........

HAMLIN & MITCHELL'S
STUPENDOUS EXTRAVAGANZA AS PRODUCED
AT THE GRAND OPERA HOUSE, CHICAGO.

BABES IN TOYLAND

BOOK AND LYRICS BY
GLEN MacDONOUGH
MUSIC BY
VICTOR HERBERT

TOYLAND

Song

50

M. WITMARK & SONS
NEW YORK   CHICAGO   LONDON
VIENNA-LEIPZIG   SAN FRANCISCO   TORONTO

Toyland.

Tom, Tom.

Lyric by
GLEN MAC DONOUGH.

Music by
VICTOR HERBERT.

Very slow and dreamily.

youve grown up my dears ____ And are as old as I. ____ You'll
youve grown up my dears ____ There comes a drear-y day ____ When

oft - en pon - der on the years That roll so swift - ly by My dears, that
'mid the locks of black ap - pears The first pale gleam of gray My dears, the

Toy - land! Toy - land! Lit _ tle girl and boy - land,

While you dwell with - in it _ You are ev - er hap - py then

Child hood's Joy - land Mys _ tic mer - ry Toy - land!

Once you pass its bor-ders you can ne'er re - turn a - gain _ When gain. _

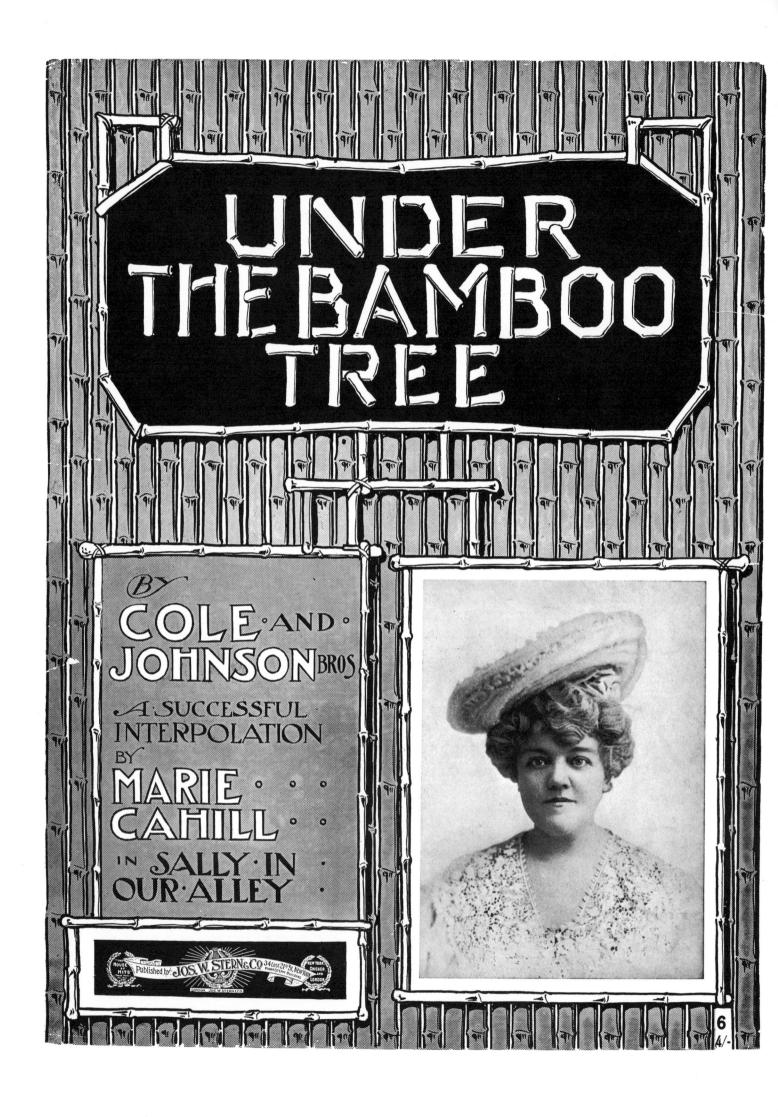

Under The Bamboo Tree.

by BOB COLE.

1. Down in the jun-gles lived a maid, Of roy-al blood though
2. And in this sim-ple jun-gle way, He wooed the maid-en
3. This lit-tle sto-ry strange but true, Is of-ten told in

dus-ky shade, A marked im-pres-sion once she made
ev'-ry day, By sing-ing what he had to say;
Ma-ta-boo, Of how this Zu-lu tried to woo

331

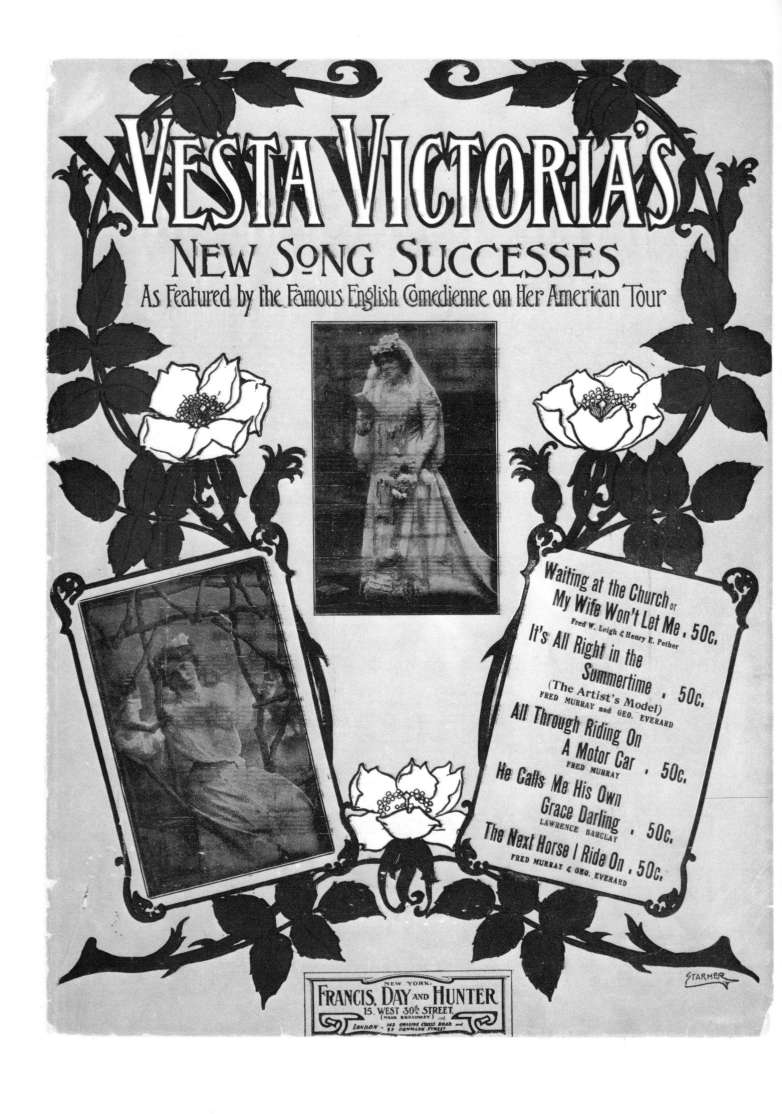

Waiting At The Church; or, My Wife Won't Let Me.

Written by
FRED W. LEIGH.

Composed by
HENRY E. PETHER.

Moderato.

Piano.

1. I'm in a nice bit of trou - ble, I con - fess,
2. Lor, what a fuss O - ba - di - ah made of me,
3. Just think of how dis - a - poin - ed I must feel.

Some - bo - dy with me has had a game, I should by now be a
When he used to take me in the park! He used to squeeze me till
I'll be go - ing cra - zy ver - y soon I've lost my hus - band the

proud and hap - py bride, But I've still got to keep my sin - gle name.
I was black and blue, When he kissed me he used to leave a mark.
one I nev - er had! _ And I dreamed so a - bout the hon - ey - moon!

I was pro - posed to by O - ba - di - ah Binks,
Each time he met me he treat - ed me to wine,
I'm look - ing out for an - oth - er O - ba - diah,

In a ver - y gen - tle - man - ly way:
Took me now and then to see the play;
I've al - read - y bought the wed - ding - ring, There's

Lent him all my mon - ey so that he could buy the home, And
Un - der - stand me right - ly, when I say he treat - ed me, It
all my lit - tle fal - the - rid - dles packed up in my box - Yes,

punc - tual - ly at twelve o' clock to - day._
was - n't him but me that used to pay.
ab - so - lute - ly two of ev - 'ry - thing.

336 *Waiting at the Church*

HARRY VON TILZER'S GREAT NOVELTY MARCH SONG

WAIT 'TILL THE SUN SHINES, NELLIE

WORDS BY
ANDREW B. STERLING
MUSIC BY
HARRY VON TILZER

HARRY VON TILZER
MUSIC PUBLISHING CO.
37 W 28ᵗᴴ Sᵀ NEW YORK. CHICAGO. FRISCO. LONDON.

5

"Wait 'till the Sun Shines, Nellie."

Words by
ANDREW B. STERLING.

Music by
HARRY VON TILZER.

pic - nic too,— at the Old Point View, It's a shame it rained to -
looked so sweet, on the big front seat, As the car sped on— its

day,_____ Then the boy drew near, kissed a - way each tear, And she
way,_____ And she whis-pered low,— "Say, you're all right Joe,— You just

poco rall.   **March Tempo.**

heard him soft - ly say._____
won my heart to - day."_____

poco rall.

CHORUS.

"Wait   'till   the sun shines, Nel-lie,   When   the clouds go

p-f

drift - ing by, We will be hap - py Nel - lie, Don't

you sigh;_____ Down lov - er's lane we'll wan - der,

Sweet-hearts you and I;_____ Wait 'till the sun shines

Nel - lie, Bye and bye."_____ bye."_____

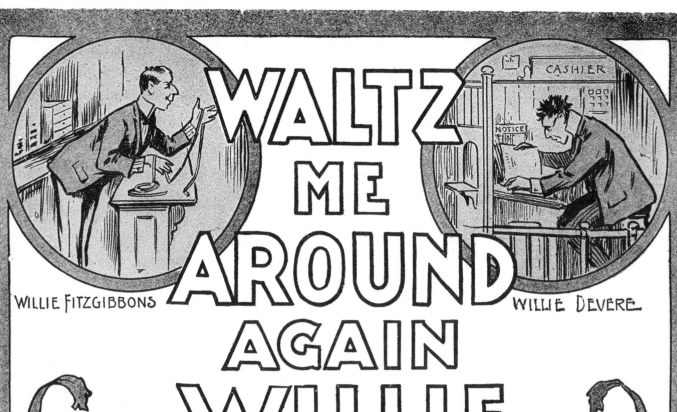

WALTZ ME AROUND AGAIN WILLIE
('ROUND-'ROUND-'ROUND)

WILLIE FITZGIBBONS

WILLIE DEVERE

WORDS BY
WILL·D·COBB

MUSIC BY
REN SHIELDS

THE AUTHOR WROTE
"GOOD-BYE DOLLY GRAY"

THE COMPOSER WROTE
"GOOD OLD SUMMERTIME"

Successfully Sung
by

Blanche Ring

in

*Charles Dillingham's
Production*

Miss Dolly Dollars

F A MILLS — 48 W 29 St

"Waltz Me Around Again Willie."

('Round, 'Round, 'Round.)

Words by
WILL D. COBB.

Music by
REN. SHIELDS.

Copyright 1906 by F. A. Mills, 48 West 29th St; N.Y.

eve - ning she'd tag him, to some dance hall drag him, And when the band
night this poor loon - ey met Mad - e - line Moon - ey, Fitz - gib - bons then

start - ed to play, _____ She'd up like a sil - ly and
shout - ed with joy, _____ "She's a good health re - gain - er, you've

grab tired Wil - lie, Steer him on the floor and she'd say: _____
got a great train - er, Just wait till she hol - lers my boy." _____

CHORUS.

"Waltz me a - round a - gain Wil - lie, a - round, a - round, a - round; _____ The

Waltz Me Around Again Willie 345

WHEN YOU WERE SWEET SIXTEEN.

SUNG WITH GREAT SUCCESS BY
BONNIE THORNTON.

ALSO SUNG WITH SUCCESS BY

JULIUS P. WITMARK.

BALLAD & REFRAIN.

WORDS & MUSIC BY

JAMES THORNTON.

5 BAND. ORCHESTRA BANJO. MANDOLIN. GUITAR.

NEW YORK
WITMARK BUILDING.
M. WITMARK & SONS
CHICAGO
SCHILLER BUILDING.
LONDON. TORONTO. HAVANA.

When You were Sweet Sixteen.

SONG AND CHORUS.

Words and Music by JAMES THORNTON.

1. When first I saw the love-light in your eye,...... And heard thy voice, like sweet-est mel-o-
2. Last night I dreamt I held your hand in mine,...... And once a-gain you were my hap-py

dy,...... Speak words of love to my en-rap-tur'd soul,......... The
bride...... I kiss'd you as I did in Auld Lang Syne,........ As

world had naught but joy in store for me.......... E'en though we're drift-ing down life's stream a-
to the church we wan-der'd side by side........ The love I bear for you can nev-er

part,.......... Your face I still can see in dream's do - main;....... I
die;.......... With - out you, I had rath - er not been born;....... And,

know that it would ease my breaking heart........ To hold you in my arms just once a-gain.....
ev - en tho' we nev - er meet a - gain,........ I love you as the sun-shine loves the morn. ...

CHORUS.

Slower.

I love you as I nev - er lov'd be - fore,........ Since

first I met you on the vil - lage green...... Come to me, or my dream of love is

o'er........ I love you as I lov'd you When you were sweet, when you were sweet sixteen.

NEW·YORK:
HARDING'S MUSIC OFFICE.

FOR SALE AT ALL MUSIC STORES.

WHERE DID YOU GET THAT HAT ?

Written & Composed by JOS. J. SULLIVAN.

Arr. by WM. LORAINE.

1. Now how I came to get this hat 'tis
2. If I go to the op-'ra house,
3. At twen-ty one I thought I would to

ve - ry strange and fun - ny: Grand-father died and left to me his
in the op-'ra sea - son, There's some-one sure to shout at me, with
my sweetheart be mar-ried; The peo - ple in the neigh-bor-hood had

prop-er-ty and mon-ey. And when the will it was read out, they
out the slightest rea-son. If I go to a "chow-der club," to
said too long we'd tar-ried. So off to church we went right quick, de-

told me straight and flat; If I would have his mon-ey, I must always wear his hat!
have a jol-ly spree;There's someone in the par-ty,who is sure to shout at me:
-termind to get wed; I had not long been in there,when the parson to me said:

CHORUS.

Where did you get that hat? Where did you get that tile?

Is-n't it a nob-by one, and just the prop-er style?

I should like to have one just the same as that! Wher-

-e'er I go they shout: "Hel-lo! Where did you get that hat?"

D.C.

* All shout.

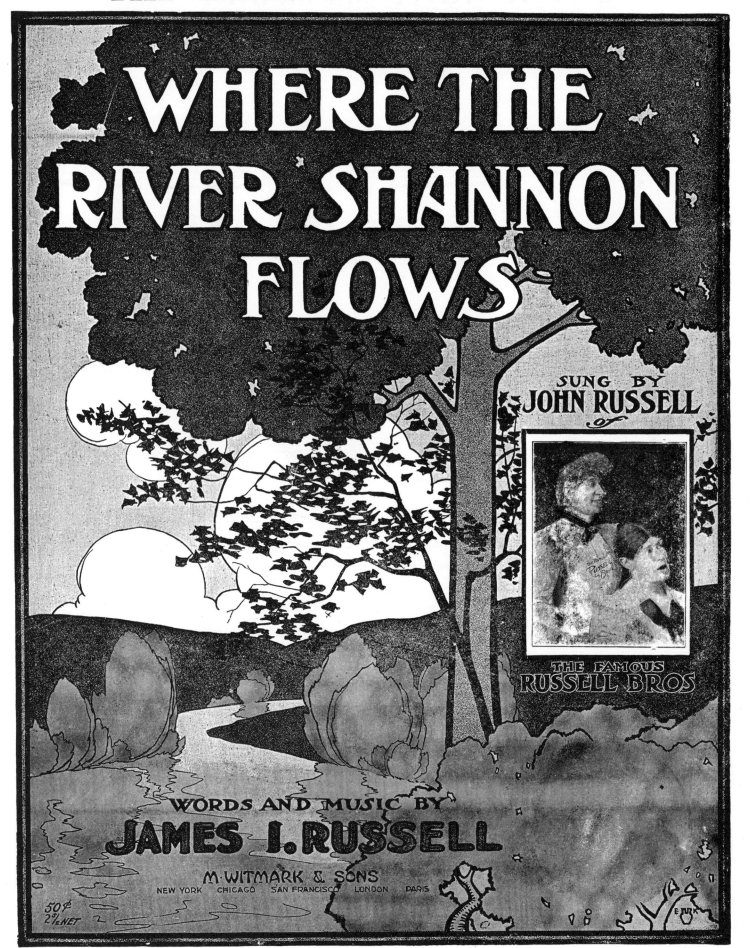

WHERE THE RIVER SHANNON FLOWS

SUNG BY
JOHN RUSSELL

THE FAMOUS
RUSSELL BROS

WORDS AND MUSIC BY
JAMES I. RUSSELL

M. WITMARK & SONS
NEW YORK   CHICAGO   SAN FRANCISCO   LONDON   PARIS

50¢
2½ NET

Where The River Shannon Flows.

JAMES I. RUSSELL.

Andante.

Piano.

There's a
Sure no

pret - ty spot in Ire - land I al - ways claim for my land, Where the
let - ter I'll be mail - ing For soon will I be sail - ing, And I'll

fair - ies and the blar - ney Will —— nev - er nev - er die. It's the
bless the ship that takes me To my dear old Er - in's shore. There I'll

land of the shil - lal - ah, My heart goes back there dai - ly To the
set - tle down for - ev - er I'll leave the old sod nev - er, And I'll

girl I left be - hind me When we kissed and said good - bye.
whis - per to my sweet-heart, "Come and take my name As - thore."

The WHISTLER AND HIS DOG

COMING! ARTHUR PRYOR AND HIS BAND.

By Arthur Pryor.

CARL FISCHER
COOPER SQUARE, NEW YORK
BOSTON:- CARL FISCHER   380 BOYLSTON ST.
CHICAGO:- L.B.MALECKI&Cº   337 S WABASH AVE

The Whistler and His Dog.

Caprice.

ARTHUR PRYOR.

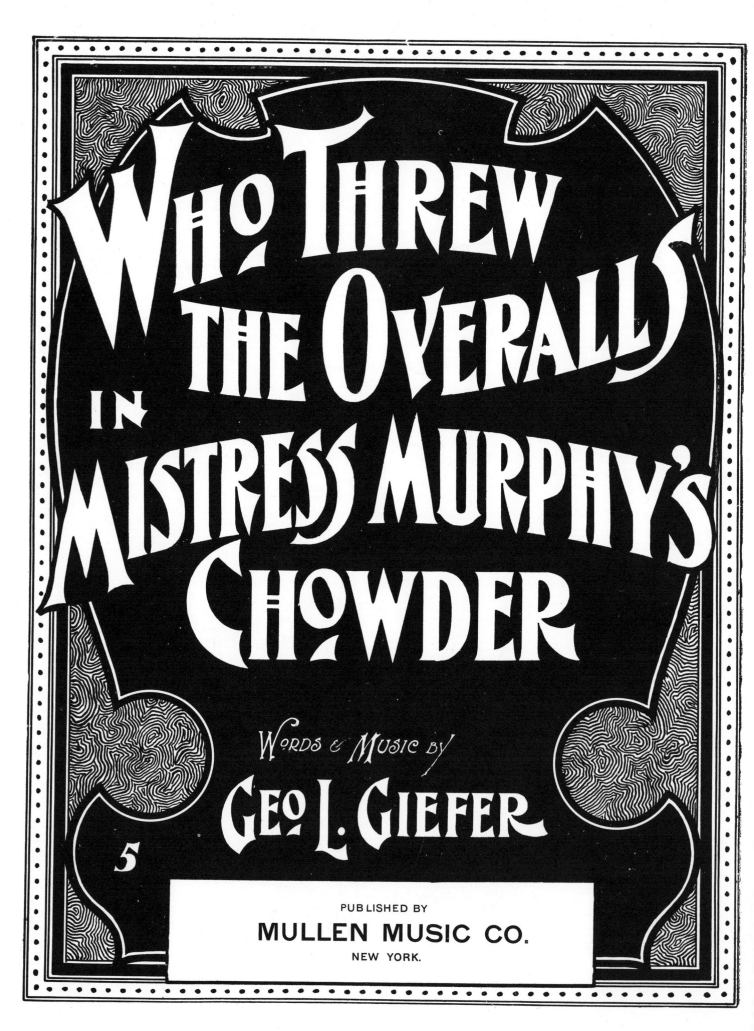

"Who Threw The Overalls In Mistress Murphy's Chowder."

Words & Music by GEO. L. GEIFER.

jumped up-on the Pi - an - o and loud - ly he did shout.
we put mu - sic to the words and sung with all our might.

CHORUS.

Who threw the ov-er-alls in Mistress Murphy's chow-der? No bo - dy

spoke so he shout-ed all the louder Its an I - rish trick that's true I can

lick the mick that threw the ov-er-alls in Mistress Murphy's chow - der

WILL YOU LOVE ME IN DECEMBER AS YOU DO IN MAY

WORDS BY
J. J. WALKER

MUSIC BY
ERNEST R. BALL

.SUNG WITH GREAT SUCCESS BY
The Spook Minstrels.

M. WITMARK & SONS
NEW YORK CHICAGO LONDON SAN FRANCISCO

Respectfully Dedicated to Mrs. Katie Oliver.

Will you love me in December
As you do in May?

Words by
J. J. WALKER.

Music by
ERNEST R. BALL.

Now in the sum-mer of life sweet-heart, You say you love but
You say the glow on my cheek sweet-heart, Is like the rose so

me, Glad - ly I give all my heart to you,
sweet; But when the bloom of fair youth has flown,

Throb-bing with ec - sta - cy. But last night I saw while a-
Then will our lips still meet? When life's set-ting sun fades a-

dream - ing, The fu - ture old and gray, And I
way dear, And all is said and done, Will your

won-dered if you'll love me then dear, Just as you do to - day.
arms still en-twine and ca - ress me, Will our hearts beat as one?

YALE
(MARCH & TWOSTEP)
BOOLA
·BY·
A·M·HIRSH

YALE 1901

Orchestra (10 Parts) and Piano 75
Full Orchestra and Piano 1.05
Military Band 50
Two Mandolins and Piano 80
Mandolin, Guitar and Piano 80
Two Mandolins and Guitar 70
Mandolin and Piano 60
Mandolin and Guitar 50
Mandolin Solo 40
Banjo Solo 40
Banjo and Piano 60

·PUBLISHED·BY·
CHAS·H·LOOMIS
833 CHAPEL STREET, NEWHAVEN CONN.

O. DITSON CO.,
Boston, Mass.

LYON & HEALY,
Chicago, Ill.

SHERMAN, CLAY & CO.,
San Francisco, Cal.

YALE BOOLA!
MARCH and TWO STEP.

A. M. HIRSH.
Arr. by G. L. Atwater, Jr.

Tempo di March.

"Here's to good old Yale."

"Boola."

Trio.

"Rah! rah! rah!"

"Bright College Years."

374   *Yale Boola*

"Boola."

"Rah! rah! rah!"

Words that can be used with

YALE BOOLA MARCH

and TWO STEP, Published and Copyrighted by CHAS. H. LOOMIS,
New Haven, Conn. ❦ ❦

ADELINA, THE YALE BOOLA GIRL.

SENTIMENTAL.

BOOLA.

Away, way down on the old Swaunee,
 Where the rippling waves are dancing to and fro,
The soft perfume from o'er the lea,
 Tells where sweet magnolia blossoms grow.
There's where my Adelina dwells,
 Mid fairy sylvan dells,
She laughs and sings the whole day through,
 Boola, Boo, Boola, 'oola, Boola, Boo!

CHORUS.

 Boola, Boola, Boola, Boola,
 Boola, Boola, Boola, Boola,
 When I meet sweet Adelina,
 Then she sings her Boola song.
 Adelina, Adelina,
 I'll be waiting Adelina,
 When the silver moon is beaming;
 Then I'll meet you, Adeline.

Her long and wavy nut-brown hair,
 Is tossing out upon the summer breeze,
Her sparkling eyes are wondrous fair,
 Her voice like the music 'mong the trees,
I ask her when she'll be my bride,
 Her head she turns aside,
And laughs and sings the whole day through,
 Boola, Boo, Boola, 'oola, Boola, Boo.—CHO.

ATHLETIC.

BOOLA.

Well, here we are; well, here we are!
 Just watch us rolling up a score.
We'll leave those fellows behind so far,
 They won't want to play us any more!
We've hope and faith in Eli Yale!
 To win we cannot fail!
Well, a Boola, Boo, Boola, Boola, Boo,
 Boola, Boo, Boola, 'oola, Boola, Boo!"

CHORUS.

 Boola, Boola, Boola, Boola,
 Boola, Boola, Boola, Boola,
 When we're through with those poor fellows,
  They will holler "Boola, Boo,
 Rah, Rah, Rah,
 Yale, Eli Yale,
 Oh, Yale, Eli Yale,
 Oh, Yale, Eli Yale,
 Oh, Yale, Eli Yale!

Now isn't it a shame, now, isn't it a shame,
 To do those fellows up so bad?
We've done it before, we can do it once more,
 Though they'll feel very very sad.
We'll roll up the score so very high,
 That you will hear them sigh,
"Boola, Boola, Boo, Boola, Boola, Boo,
 Boola, Boo, Boola, 'oola, Boola, Boo!"

COLLEGE.

YALE BOOLA, TRIO:

Bright College Years with pleasure rife,
The shortest gladdest years of life,
How swiftly are ye gliding by,
Oh why doth time so quickly fly?
The seasons come, the seasons go,
The earth is green, or white with snow,
But time and change shall nought avail
To break the friendships formed at Yale!

We all must leave this College Home,
About the stormy world to roam,
But though the mighty ocean's tide,
Should us from dear old Yale divide,
As round the oak the ivy twines,
The clinging tendrils of its vines,
So are our hearts close bound to Yale,
By ties of love that ne'er shall fail.

In after years should troubles rise,
To cloud the blue of sunny skies,
How bright will seem thro' memory's haze,
The happy, golden by-gone days,
Oh, let us strive that ever we
May let these word our watch-cry be,
Where'er upon life's sea we sail,
"For God, for Country and for Yale!"

FROM YALE SONGS BY PERMISSION.

All the words on this Sheet can be sung to the Yale Boola March and fit exactly if accented properly.

The YANKEE DOODLE BOY

ONE OF THE
MUSICAL HITS *from*
GEO. M. COHAN'S
LATEST PLAY

"LITTLE
JOHNNY
JONES"

Words &
Music by
GEO. M. COHAN

THE
YANKEE
DOODLE COMEDIAN

F. A. MILLS
48 WEST 29TH ST.
NEW YORK

"The Yankee Doodle Boy."

GEO. M. COHAN.

I'm the kid that's all the can - dy,
Fa - ther's name was Hez - i - ki - ah,

I'm a Yan - kee Doo - dle Dan - dy, I'm glad I am, —
Moth - er's name was Ann Ma - ri - a, Yanks through and through.

CHO. (So's Un - cle Sam.) I'm a real live Yan - kee Doo - dle,
CHO. (Red, White and Blue.) Fa - ther was so Yan - kee - heart - ed,

Made my name and fame and boo - dle, Just like Mis - ter Doo - dle did, by
When the Span - ish war was start - ed, He slipped on his un - i - form and

rid - ing on a po - ny. I love to lis - ten to the
hopped up - on a po - ny. My moth - er's moth - er was a

Dix - ey strain, "I long to see the girl I left be - hind me;"And
Yan - kee true, My fa - ther's fa - ther was a Yan - kee too; And

that ain't a josh, She's a Yan-kee, by gosh. *CHO.* (Oh,
that's go - ing some, For the Yan-kees, by gum. *CHO.* (Oh,

say   can   you   see _____ An - y -
say   can   you   see _____ An - y -

thing a - bout a Yan - kee that's a phon - - ey?)
thing a - bout my ped - i - gree that's phon - - ey?)

CHORUS.

I'm a Yan - kee Doo - dle Dan - dy, A
Yan - kee Doo - dle, do or die; A
real live nep - hew of my Un - cle Sam's,
Born on the Fourth of Ju - ly. I've

YOU'RE A GRAND OLD FLAG

A SONG-HIT FROM THE LATEST MUSICAL PLAY

GEORGE WASHINGTON JR.

WRITTEN AND COMPOSED BY

GEO. M. COHAN

5

F. A. MILLS
48 WEST 29th ST.
NEW YORK

"You're A Grand Old Flag."

GEO. M. COHAN.

feel - ing comes a - steal - ing and it sets my brain a reel - ing, When I'm
crank - y, hank - y pank - y, I'm a dead square hon - est Yan - kee, And I'm

list - 'ning to the mu - sic of a mil - i - ta - ry band. An - y
migh - ty proud of that old flag that flies for Un - cle Sam. Though I

tune like "Yan-kee Doo-dle" simp-ly sets me off my noo-dle, It's that
don't be-lieve in rav-ing ev-'ry time I see it wav-ing, There's a

pa-tri-ot-ic some-thing that no one can un-der-stand.
chill runs up my back that makes me glad I'm what I am.

Chorus.   **Solo.**

"Way down South in the land of cot-ton," mel - - o - dy un-
Here's a land with a mil-lion sol-diers, that's_____ if we should

                                               Chorus.

tir - ing,_____ Ain't that in-spir-ing!_____ Hur - rah! Hur-
need 'em,_____ We'll fight for free-dom!_____ Hur - rah! Hur-

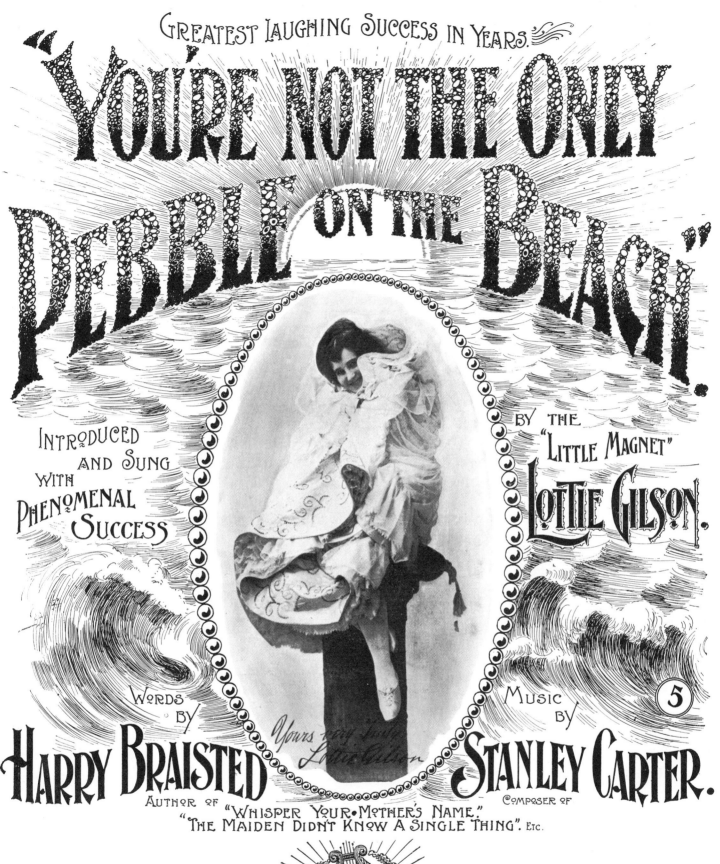

YOU'RE NOT THE ONLY PEBBLE ON THE BEACH.

Words by Harry Braisted.

Music by Stanley Carter.

1. When you see a pret-ty maid-en who has just turn'd sev-en-teen, You
2. While on board a crowded horse-car, on a warm and sul-try day, I
3. I live op-po-site a maid-en, and I know her stea-dy beau, He

think you'd like to win her for your wife;........ Don't start the game by saying she's the
saw a maid-en o-ver-come with heat;........ She stood there fifteen minutes, while a
tells me that she loves no one but him;........ He buys her all her dresses and her

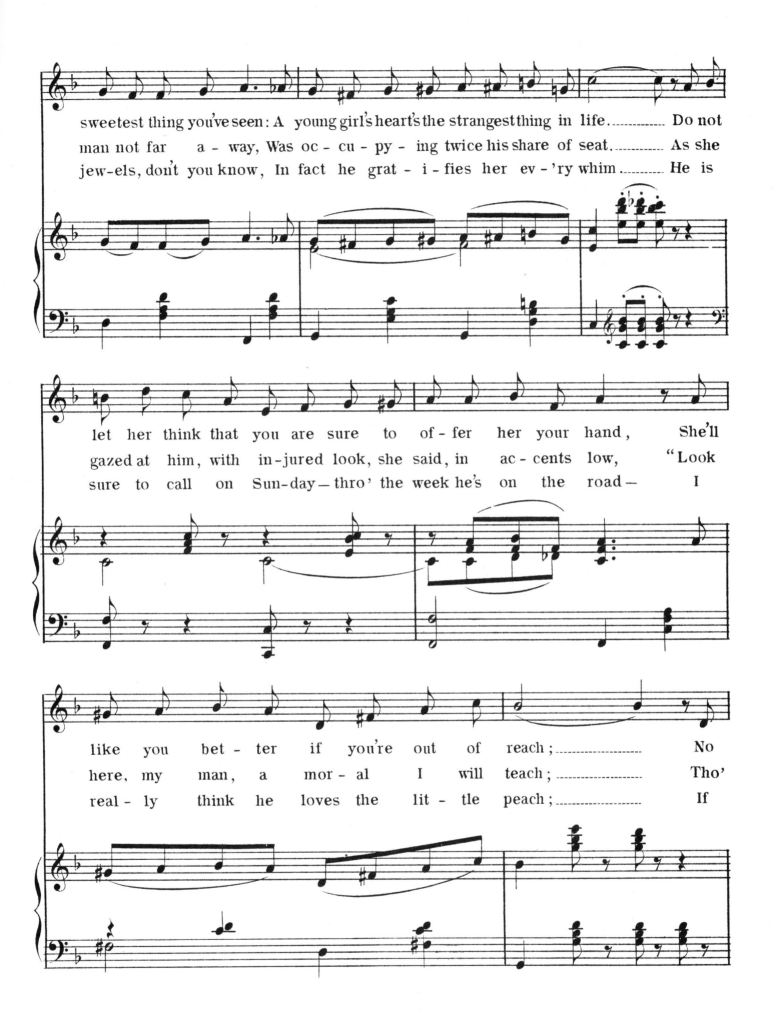

sweetest thing you've seen: A young girl's heart's the strangest thing in life............ Do not
man not far a - way, Was oc - cu - py - ing twice his share of seat............ As she
jew-els, don't you know, In fact he grat - i - fies her ev - 'ry whim.......... He is

let her think that you are sure to of - fer her your hand, She'll
gazed at him, with in-jured look, she said, in ac - cents low, "Look
sure to call on Sun-day—thro' the week he's on the road— I

like you bet - ter if you're out of reach; _____ No
here, my man, a mor - al I will teach; _____ Tho'
real - ly think he loves the lit - tle peach; _____ If

matter how you love her, give the girl to un-der-stand She's
you have paid your nick-el, there are oth-ers, don't you know, You're
he could see the rush on Mon-day nights, I think he'd know He's

not the on-ly peb-ble on the beach!....................
not the on-ly peb-ble on the beach!"....................
not the on-ly peb-ble on the beach!....................

CHORUS.

1. She's not the on-ly pebble on the beach! That is the sort of les-son
2. "You're not the on-ly pebble on the beach! For there are oth-ers," said the
3. He's not the on-ly pebble on the beach! She has a hundred more with

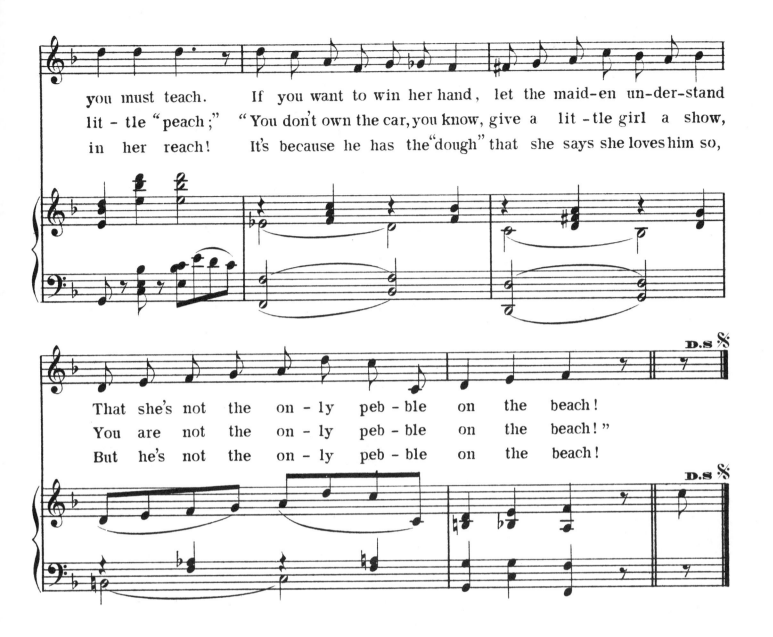

you must teach. If you want to win her hand, let the maid-en un-der-stand
lit - tle "peach;" "You don't own the car, you know, give a lit - tle girl a show,
in her reach! It's because he has the "dough" that she says she loves him so,

That she's not the on - ly peb - ble on the beach!
You are not the on - ly peb - ble on the beach!"
But he's not the on - ly peb - ble on the beach!

D.S 𝄋

4.

I was listening to a talk between two men, the other day,
 The conversation ran on married life;
And I was interested as I heard one of them say
 He thought that every man should have a wife.
For he said, "My friend, I'm married, and I'm happy as can be;
 But don't let it go farther, I beseech!
I haven't seen my darling wife in years, 'twixt you and me,
 And there are others like me on the beach!"

Chorus.

There are a lot of others on the beach!
And you can take advice from what I preach:
  When on married life you start,
  Take a "tip" and live apart,—
There are lots of other pebbles on the beach!

Sung with Great Success by
GEO. DONALDSON
OF THE SYMPHONY QUARTETTE

YOU'RE THE FLOWER OF MY HEART,
SWEET ADELINE

Ballad & Refrain.

WORDS BY
RICHARD H. GERARD.

MUSIC BY
HENRY W. ARMSTRONG.

M. WITMARK & SONS
NEW YORK   CHICAGO   LONDON   SAN FRANCISCO.
JOSEF WEINBERGER, LEIPZIG AND VIENNA
ALLAN & CO. MELBOURNE, AUSTRALIA
CANADIAN-AMERICAN MUSIC CO. LTD. TORONTO

50¢
2/- NET

You're the Flower of My Heart, Sweet Adeline.

Words by RICHARD H. GERARD. Music by HARRY ARMSTRONG.

In the eve-ning when I sit a-lone a dream-ing____ Of days gone
I can see your smil-ing face as when we wand-ered____ Down by the

by, love____ to me so dear. There's a
brook-side____ just you and I, And it

pic-ture that in fan-cy 'oft ap-pear-ing,____ Brings back the
seems so real at times 'till I a-wak'-en____ To find all

CHORUS.

Sweet A - del - ine, ___ My A - del - ine ___ At night, Dear-
heart ___ For you I pine, ___ In all my
dreams, ___ Your fair face beams, ___ You're the
flow - er of my heart, Sweet A - de - line.

"As Sung by Miss Etta Butler

YOU TELL ME YOUR DREAM, I'LL TELL YOU MINE.

Words by
SEYMOUR RICE
AND
ALBERT H. BROWN

Music by
CHAS. N. DANIELS

5

Daniels Russell & Boone   St. Louis, Mo.

"You tell me your dream, I'll tell you mine".

Words by
SEYMOUR RICE and ALBERT H. BROWN.

Music by
CHAS. N. DANIELS.

lone on the din-ing room floor;_____ The girl of a dream had been
Ma-ry then blush-ing-ly said;_____ Time they say brings many
grief has dis-pelled their bright dream;_____ For Ma-ry his kind lov-ing

talk _ ing, but re-fused with a toss of her head _____ To tell it
chang _ es, but their love no change ev-er knew _____ And so they were
help _ mate, had yes-ter-day passed a _ way _____ And in sor-row Tom

all to her play _ mate, un-til he coax-ing-ly said._____
hap-pi-ly mar _ ried, The dream of their child-hood came true._____
thinks of the morn _ ing, When in child-hood to her he did say._____